I0446250

Data Structures and AI: Building Intelligent Systems

First Edition

J. B. P. Brown

by

A RedMars Product – written by J. B. P. Brown, Miami, Florida, United States
www.RedMars.com

Information on this title can be found at:
www.redmars.com/PolyBitz
© J. B. P. Brown – RedMars

Published 2023

ISBN: 9798867500443

For any corrections or inquiries to the content of this publication, please contact RedMars directly through
www.RedMars.com/contact

Table of Contents

Introduction: Unveiling the Power of Data Structures

In the ever-evolving landscape of computer science, data structures and artificial intelligence (AI) stand as the cornerstones of efficient and organized information handling and intelligent problem-solving. Whether you're a novice programmer looking to grasp the fundamentals or a seasoned developer seeking to optimize your code while incorporating AI, understanding the interplay of data structures and AI is a pivotal skill.

This book delves into the world of data structures and their seamless integration with AI, providing you with a comprehensive guide to mastering them in two of the most influential programming languages: Python and C++. Python's simplicity and readability, coupled with C++'s performance and power, offer a dynamic duo for exploring and implementing data structures in the context of AI-driven projects.

The Importance of Data Structures and AI:

At the heart of every software application and algorithm, you'll find data structures. They define how data is organized, stored, and manipulated, impacting the efficiency and functionality of your code. With the inclusion of AI, data structures play a crucial role in handling and processing data for machine learning, natural language processing, computer vision, and more. Whether you're working on a small personal project or a large-scale enterprise system, choosing the right data structure, especially when integrating AI components, can make a world of difference.

Why Python and C++ for Data Structures and AI:

Python's expressive syntax and extensive standard library make it an ideal choice for rapid development and prototyping in the field of AI, while C++ excels in performance-critical AI applications. By mastering data structures in both languages and their application to AI, you'll have a versatile skill set to tackle a wide range of challenges, from AI model development to optimizing data pipelines.

Overview of the Book:

In the following chapters, we'll embark on a journey through the realm of data structures, AI algorithms, and their synergistic relationship. We'll begin with the fundamentals, gradually progressing to more complex structures and algorithmic techniques, with a specific focus on their use in AI applications. Along the way, you'll not only learn how to implement and use these structures in Python and C++ but also understand the principles behind them and how they drive AI.

Whether you're a student, a software engineer, or a data scientist, this book is designed to equip you with the knowledge and practical skills needed to create efficient and elegant solutions to real-world problems, leveraging the combined power of data structures and AI. By the end of this journey, you'll be well-prepared to harness the potential of data structures and AI in your programming endeavors. So, let's dive into the fascinating world of data structures and AI and unlock their potential in Python and C++. Your adventure begins here!

Python serves as an excellent starting point for our exploration of data structures. This chapter lays the foundation by covering the basics of Python programming and the fundamental data structures built into the language.

2.1 Basics of Python

Python, a versatile and beginner-friendly programming language, serves as an excellent starting point for our exploration of data structures. In this section, we will delve into the foundational aspects of Python.

Python has earned its place as a popular and widely-used language for a variety of reasons. Its history traces back to the late 1980s when Guido van Rossum created the language. Python's design philosophy emphasizes code readability and a straightforward syntax, which makes it approachable for newcomers while ensuring experienced developers can work efficiently. These attributes have contributed to Python's reputation as one of the most beginner-friendly languages. Moreover, Python is not confined to specific domains; it has a robust standard library and a vibrant community, which means it can be applied in web development, data analysis, scientific computing, artificial intelligence, and more. As we delve deeper into data structures in Python, you'll discover the language's adaptability and versatility.

To master data structures in Python, it's essential to begin with the basics. We'll start by discussing fundamental Python concepts, including variables, data types, and basic operations. Variables serve as containers for storing data, and Python allows you to use meaningful names for these containers. Python supports various data types, including integers, floating-point numbers, strings, and more. Understanding these types and their uses is essential as they form the building blocks for data structures. Python also offers a range of basic operations, from arithmetic to string manipulation. Familiarity with these operations is critical for implementing and working with data structures effectively.

As we progress through the book, this foundational knowledge will serve as a solid platform for exploring Python's data structures and their implementations. Whether you're new to Python or looking to reinforce your skills, this section aims to help you navigate the Python programming landscape with ease and confidence. Python's clean and readable syntax, coupled with a rich standard library, provides a comfortable environment for developing a wide range of applications, from web development to data science and machine learning. By mastering the basics of Python, you'll be well-prepared to dive deeper into data structures and algorithms in this versatile language.

2.2 Lists and Tuples

In Python, lists and tuples are fundamental data structures used for organizing and managing collections of elements. They serve as versatile containers and play essential roles in data manipulation.

Lists are ordered collections of elements enclosed in square brackets (`[]`). They are versatile and can hold a mix of different data types, making them a popular choice for various applications. Lists are mutable, which means you can add, remove, or modify elements after creating them. For example, a list can hold integers, strings, and even other lists. To access elements in a list, you use zero-based indexing. Python's flexibility in handling lists makes them indispensable for a wide range of tasks, from managing data to implementing algorithms. Understanding lists is a fundamental step in mastering data structures in Python.

Tuples are similar to lists, but with a crucial difference: they are immutable, meaning their elements cannot be changed after creation. Tuples are created by enclosing elements in parentheses ('()'). This immutability provides advantages in scenarios where data should not be altered. For example, you might use tuples to represent coordinates, dates, or any data that should remain constant. The immutability of tuples ensures data integrity and can be more efficient in certain situations compared to lists. While they don't offer the same flexibility as lists, tuples are invaluable for protecting and efficiently storing data.

```python
1   # Define a Tuple
2   fruits_tuple = ('apple', 'banana', 'cherry', 'date')
3
4   # Accessing Tuple Elements
5   print("First fruit:", fruits_tuple[0])   # Output: First fruit: apple
6   print("Last fruit:", fruits_tuple[-1])   # Output: Last fruit: date
7
8   # Iterate through a Tuple
9   for fruit in fruits_tuple:
10      print(fruit)
11
12  # Define a List
13  colors_list = ['red', 'green', 'blue', 'yellow']
14
15  # Accessing List Elements
16  print("First color:", colors_list[0])   # Output: First color: red
17  print("Last color:", colors_list[-1])   # Output: Last color: yellow
18
19  # Iterate through a List
20  for color in colors_list:
21      print(color)
22
23  # Modifying a List (Lists are mutable)
24  colors_list[0] = 'purple'
25  print(colors_list)  # Output: ['purple', 'green', 'blue', 'yellow']
26
27  '''
28  Modifying a Tuple (Tuples are immutable - this will raise an error)
29  fruits_tuple[0] = 'orange'  # TypeError: 'tuple' object does not
30  support item assignment
31  '''
```

Figure 2.1

16

In Figure 2.1:

- We define a tuple called `fruits_tuple` with four elements.
- We access tuple elements using indexing and negative indexing.
- We demonstrate how to iterate through a tuple using a `for` loop.
- We define a list called `colors_list` with four elements.
- We access list elements using indexing.
- We demonstrate how to iterate through a list using a `for` loop.
- We modify the first element of the list to change its value.
- We attempt to modify the first element of the tuple (commented out because tuples are immutable, and this would result in a `TypeError`).

Again, note that Tuples are immutable, meaning their elements cannot be changed after creation, while lists are mutable, allowing you to modify their contents.

Both lists and tuples support common operations, such as indexing, slicing, concatenation, and repetition. Understanding these operations is vital for working with these data structures effectively. You can use indexing to access individual elements by their position, while slicing enables you to extract sub-lists or subsequences. Combining lists or tuples is achieved through concatenation, and repetition allows you to create longer sequences by repeating elements.

As we dive deeper into data structures in Python, lists and tuples will frequently come into play. Their flexibility, combined with their unique characteristics of mutability and immutability, provide the foundation for building more complex data structures. You'll learn how to leverage lists and tuples in various contexts, from creating dynamic arrays to organizing data efficiently. This knowledge will serve as a valuable asset as we continue our exploration of data structures in Python.

2.3 Dictionaries and Sets

Dictionaries and sets are versatile data structures in Python, each serving a unique purpose in organizing and manipulating data. In this section, we'll explore their characteristics, applications, and how to work with them.

Dictionaries are collections of key-value pairs, enclosed in curly braces (`{}`). They are known by different names in other programming languages, such as associative arrays or maps. Dictionaries are designed for efficient data retrieval based on keys, making them ideal for scenarios where fast access to values is essential. Keys must be unique and immutable, such as strings or numbers, while values can be of any data type. Dictionaries are mutable, allowing you to add, update, or remove key-value pairs. This data structure is essential for tasks like creating data caches, implementing data-driven applications, or organizing configurations.

Sets, on the other hand, are collections of unique elements, also enclosed in curly braces (`{}`). Sets ensure that there are no duplicate values, making them useful for storing distinct items. Sets support common set operations like union, intersection, and difference, which can be helpful in various applications, including finding common elements in two datasets or removing duplicates from a list. Sets are mutable, allowing you to add or remove elements. You can also create frozen sets, which are immutable and useful when you need to ensure the data remains constant.

```python
1   # Define a Dictionary
2   person_info = {
3       'name': 'Alice',
4       'age': 30,
5       'city': 'New York'
6   }
7
8   # Accessing Dictionary Elements
9   print("Name:", person_info['name'])   # Output: Name: Alice
10  print("Age:", person_info['age'])      # Output: Age: 30
11
12  # Iterate through a Dictionary
13  for key, value in person_info.items():
14      print(key, ":", value)
15
16  # Modify a Dictionary
17  person_info['city'] = 'Los Angeles'
18  # Output: {'name': 'Alice', 'age': 30, 'city': 'Los Angeles'}
19  print(person_info)
20
21  # Define a Set
22  unique_numbers = {1, 2, 3, 4, 5, 5, 4}
23
24  # Accessing Set Elements
25  # Output: Set of unique numbers: {1, 2, 3, 4, 5}
26  print("Set of unique numbers:", unique_numbers)
27
28  # Iterate through a Set
29  for number in unique_numbers:
30      print(number)
31
32  # Add elements to a Set (Sets automatically eliminate duplicates)
33  unique_numbers.add(6)
34  print(unique_numbers)   # Output: {1, 2, 3, 4, 5, 6}
35
36  # Remove an element from a Set
37  unique_numbers.remove(3)
38  print(unique_numbers)   # Output: {1, 2, 4, 5, 6}
```

Figure 2.2

In Figure 2.3.1:

- We define a dictionary called `person_info` with key-value pairs representing a person's information.
- We access dictionary elements using keys.

- We demonstrate how to iterate through a dictionary using a `for` loop and the `items()` method.
- We modify the 'city' value in the dictionary.
- We define a set called `unique_numbers` with unique integer elements.
- We access set elements and notice that duplicates are automatically eliminated.
- We iterate through a set using a `for` loop.
- We add an element to the set using the `add()` method.
- We remove an element from the set using the `remove()` method.

Dictionaries and sets find applications in a wide array of practical scenarios. Dictionaries are invaluable for creating lookup tables, implementing efficient data searching, and organizing data for data analysis or configuration management. Sets are indispensable for working with unique values, handling membership tests, and performing set operations efficiently. Whether you need to count word occurrences in a text document or identify unique elements in a list, dictionaries and sets are the go-to data structures.

Understanding the efficiency of dictionaries and sets is crucial. Dictionaries provide constant-time average complexity for key-based operations, making them efficient for searching, while sets excel in maintaining unique elements with O(1) time complexity for membership tests. We'll explore these efficiency considerations and delve into real-world use cases for both data structures.

As we progress through the book, dictionaries and sets will continue to be valuable tools in your Python programming toolkit. Their efficiency and unique capabilities make them essential for solving a wide range of data manipulation challenges. You'll learn how to create, modify, and retrieve data from dictionaries and sets, and explore scenarios where they shine. This knowledge will empower you to work with more complex data structures and tackle various data-driven tasks in Python.

2.4 Time and Space Complexity

Understanding the time and space complexity of algorithms and data structures is crucial for assessing their efficiency and making informed decisions when designing and implementing solutions. In this section, we'll delve into the concepts of time and space complexity and how to analyze them.

2.4.1 Time Complexity

Time complexity refers to the amount of time an algorithm takes to complete its task as a function of the input size. It quantifies the number of basic operations (usually expressed as a count of key comparisons, assignments, or arithmetic operations) performed by the algorithm in relation to the size of the input. Time complexity is often expressed using "Big O" notation (e.g., $O(1)$, $O(\log n)$, $O(n)$, $O(n \log n)$, $O(n^2)$).

The below descriptions contain code samples, demonstrating each time and space complexity. Try to work through how these come to the specified complexities.

O(1) (Constant Time): Operations with constant time complexity always take the same amount of time, regardless of the input size. Accessing an element by index in a list or performing arithmetic operations are examples of $O(1)$ operations.

```
1    def constant_time_example(arr):
2        return arr[0]
3
4    arr = [1, 2, 3, 4, 5]
5    result = constant_time_example(arr)
6    print(result)  # Output: 1
```
Figure 2.3

O(log n) (Logarithmic Time): Algorithms with logarithmic time complexity grow slower as the input size increases. Binary search is a classic example of $O(\log n)$ complexity.

```
1   def binary_search(arr, target):
2       low, high = 0, len(arr) - 1
3       while low <= high:
4           mid = (low + high) // 2
5           if arr[mid] == target:
6               return mid
7           elif arr[mid] < target:
8               low = mid + 1
9           else:
10              high = mid - 1
11      return -1
12
13  arr = [1, 2, 3, 4, 5, 6, 7, 8, 9, 10]
14  target = 7
15  result = binary_search(arr, target)
16  print(result)  # Output: 6
```

Figure 2.4

O(n) (Linear Time): Linear time complexity signifies that the algorithm's running time increases linearly with the size of the input. Traversing an array or list is an example of O(n) complexity.

```
1   def linear_time_example(arr):
2       total = 0
3       for num in arr:
4           total += num
5       return total
6
7   arr = [1, 2, 3, 4, 5]
8   result = linear_time_example(arr)
9   print(result)  # Output: 15
```

Figure 2.5

O(n log n) (Linearithmic Time): This complexity is often seen in efficient sorting algorithms like merge sort and quicksort.

22

```
1    def n_log_n_time_example(arr):
2        return sorted(arr)
3
4    arr = [5, 1, 3, 4, 2]
5    result = n_log_n_time_example(arr)
6    print(result)  # Output: [1, 2, 3, 4, 5]
```
Figure 2.6

O(n^2) (Quadratic Time): Algorithms with quadratic time complexity have a running time proportional to the square of the input size. Nested loops are typical culprits for O(n^2) complexity.

```
1    def quadratic_time_example(arr):
2        result = []
3        for i in arr:
4            for j in arr:
5                result.append(i * j)
6        return result
7
8    arr = [1, 2, 3]
9    result = quadratic_time_example(arr)
10   print(result)
```
Figure 2.7

2.4.2 Space Complexity

Space complexity measures the amount of memory space an algorithm or data structure uses as a function of the input size. It quantifies how additional memory requirements grow with the size of the input. Space complexity is also expressed using Big O notation.

O(1) (Constant Space): Algorithms with constant space complexity use a fixed amount of memory, independent of the input size. Variables or a fixed-size array are examples of O(1) space complexity.

```
1   def constant_space_example():
2       a = 1
3       b = 2
4       return a + b
5
6   result = constant_space_example()
```
Figure 2.8

O(n) (Linear Space): Linear space complexity means that memory usage grows linearly with the input size. Storing a list of values proportional to the input size demonstrates O(n) space complexity.

```
1   def linear_space_example(n):
2       arr = [0] * n
3       return arr
4
5   n = 10
6   result = linear_space_example(n)
```
Figure 2.9

O(n^2) (Quadratic Space): Quadratic space complexity indicates that memory usage increases with the square of the input size. Matrices and multi-dimensional arrays often exhibit O(n^2) space complexity.

```
1   def quadratic_space_example(n):
2       matrix = [[0 for _ in range(n)] for _ in range(n)]
3       return matrix
4
5   n = 4
6   result = quadratic_space_example(n)
```
Figure 2.10

O(log n) (Logarithmic Space): Algorithms with logarithmic space complexity use an amount of memory that grows logarithmically with the input size.

```
1  ∨ def recursive_log_space(n):
2  ∨     if n <= 1:
3            return n
4        return recursive_log_space(n-1) + recursive_log_space(n-2)
5
6     n = 5
7     result = recursive_log_space(n)
```

Figure 2.11

Analyzing the time and space complexity of your algorithms and data structures is essential for optimizing your code and choosing the right tools for the job. It helps you understand how an algorithm's performance scales with input size and whether it's suitable for large datasets or time-critical tasks. As you explore various data structures and algorithms in this book, you'll gain a better understanding of their associated complexities and be better equipped to make informed decisions when solving real-world problems.

Chapter 3: C++ Fundamentals

In this chapter, we'll shift our focus to C++, a powerful and versatile programming language, and explore its fundamental features and data structures. Whether you're new to C++ or looking to apply your existing knowledge to data structures, this chapter will provide the necessary foundation.

3.1 Introduction to C++

C++ is a powerful and versatile programming language known for its efficiency and performance. In this section, we'll provide an overview of C++ and highlight its significance as a language for data structures and algorithms.

C++ is an extension of the C programming language, adding object-oriented features while retaining C's low-level capabilities. This combination of features makes C++ an ideal choice for developing data structures and algorithms. C++ is known for its performance and efficiency, making it a popular language in fields where fast execution is critical, such as game development, system programming, and scientific computing.

- Efficiency: C++ provides control over memory management, making it possible to optimize data structures for performance. It offers pointers, manual memory allocation, and direct access to hardware resources when necessary.

- Object-Oriented: C++ supports object-oriented programming, which allows for modular and organized code. This is valuable when designing complex data structures and algorithms.

- Standard Template Library (STL): C++ includes the STL, which provides a collection of data structures and algorithms that can be readily used. The STL simplifies common programming tasks, including sorting, searching, and managing containers like vectors, lists, and queues.

- Multi-Paradigm: C++ supports multiple programming paradigms, including procedural, object-oriented, and generic programming. This flexibility enables developers to choose the most appropriate approach for a given task.

- Compile-Time Type Checking: C++ performs strong type checking at compile time, which helps catch errors before the program runs, leading to more robust code.

3.1.1 Exploring C++ Basics

Before diving into data structures and algorithms in C++, it's essential to grasp the basics. C++ uses a similar syntax to C and other C-style languages. You'll work with variables, data types, loops, and conditionals. Functions and classes are crucial components for structuring code in C++, and understanding pointers and memory management is essential for more advanced topics.

In the sections that follow, we'll delve into C++'s role in data structures and algorithms. C++ allows you to create efficient and optimized implementations of various data structures, which are critical in solving complex problems and building high-performance applications. Whether you're new to C++ or looking to enhance your programming skills, this section lays the foundation for your journey into the world of data structures and algorithms in C++.

3.2 Arrays and Vectors

Arrays and vectors are fundamental data structures used to store collections of elements in C++. In this section, we'll explore these data structures, their characteristics, and how to work with them effectively.

27

3.2.1 Understanding Arrays

An array is a fixed-size collection of elements, all of the same data type. Arrays are one of the simplest and most commonly used data structures in C++. They offer efficient memory management, as the elements are stored in contiguous memory locations, allowing for fast random access. However, arrays have a fixed size determined at compile time, which can limit their flexibility.

3.2.2 Defining and Accessing Arrays

In C++, you define an array by specifying its data type and size. For example, to create an array of integers with five elements:

```
1    int myArray[5];
```
Figure 3.1

You can access array elements using zero-based indexing, like this:

```
1    myArray[0] = 42; // Assign 42 to the first element
2    int value = myArray[2]; // Retrieve the third element's value
```
Figure 3.2

3.2.3 Understanding Vectors

Vectors are dynamic arrays provided by the Standard Template Library (STL). Unlike traditional arrays, vectors can grow or shrink dynamically during runtime. This flexibility makes vectors an attractive choice when you need to work with collections of elements whose size may change. Vectors also provide several useful member functions, making them easier to work with.

3.2.4 Using Vectors

To use vectors, include the necessary header and declare a vector of a specific data type:

28

```
1    #include <vector>
2    std::vector<int> myVector;
```
Figure 3.3

You can add elements to a vector using the `push_back` method, and vectors automatically resize as needed:

```
1    myVector.push_back(10);
2    myVector.push_back(20);
3    myVector.push_back(30);
```
Figure 3.4

You can access vector elements similarly to arrays:

```
1    int value = myVector[1]; // Retrieve the second element's value
```
Figure 3.5

3.2.5 Common Operations

Both arrays and vectors support common operations, such as accessing elements, adding elements, and iterating through the collection. They differ in how they handle size constraints. Arrays have a fixed size, and adding elements beyond that size can lead to undefined behavior. Vectors, on the other hand, automatically manage their size, making them safer and more flexible.

3.2.6 Efficiency and Use Cases

Arrays offer efficient memory usage, and their size is known at compile time. They are suitable for situations where a fixed-size collection is sufficient. Vectors, with their dynamic sizing, are a more versatile choice when the number of elements can change during program execution. Vectors may have a slight overhead due to dynamic resizing but provide ease of use and safety in return.

3.3 Maps and Sets

Maps and sets are versatile data structures used for organizing and retrieving data in C++. In this section, we'll explore these data structures, their characteristics, and how to work with them effectively.

3.3.1 Understanding Maps

A map is an associative container that stores key-value pairs. Each key is unique and associated with a specific value. In C++, the `std::map` and `std::unordered_map` classes provide efficient implementations of maps. A `std::map` is typically implemented as a red-black tree, while a `std::unordered_map` uses a hash table.

3.3.2 Defining and Using Maps

To create a map in C++, you specify the key and value types within angle brackets, like this:

```
1    #include <map>
2    std::map<std::string, int> myMap;
```
Figure 3.6

You can add key-value pairs to the map using the `insert` function:

```
1    myMap.insert(std::pair<std::string, int>("Alice", 30));
2    myMap.insert(std::pair<std::string, int>("Bob", 25));
```
Figure 3.7

You can also use the square bracket notation for accessing values by key:

```
1    int aliceAge = myMap["Alice"];
```
Figure 3.8

3.3.3 Understanding Sets

A set is a collection of unique elements. In C++, the `std::set` and `std::unordered_set` classes provide efficient implementations of sets. A `std::set` is typically implemented as a red-black tree, while a `std::unordered_set` uses a hash table.

3.3.4 Using Sets

To create a set in C++, you specify the element type within angle brackets, like this:

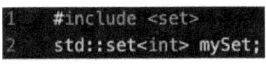

```
1    #include <set>
2    std::set<int> mySet;
```

Figure 3.9

You can add elements to the set using the `insert` function:

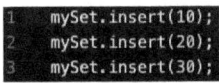

```
1    mySet.insert(10);
2    mySet.insert(20);
3    mySet.insert(30);
```

Figure 3.10

You can check if an element exists in the set and perform various set operations, such as union and intersection.

3.3.5 Common Operations

Maps and sets support common operations such as inserting elements, searching for elements, and iterating through the collection. They excel at scenarios where uniqueness and efficient lookups are required. Unlike arrays and vectors, maps and sets don't allow duplicate elements.

3.3.6 Efficiency and Use Cases

Maps and sets are efficient data structures for storing unique elements and associating values with keys. They provide fast lookups and are suitable for situations where you need to maintain a collection of distinct elements. Maps are particularly useful when you need to associate additional data (the values) with the elements, while sets are excellent for scenarios where uniqueness is the primary concern.

3.4 Complexity Analysis in C++

In C++, you can analyze the time and space complexity of your code by examining loops, function calls, and memory allocations. Understanding these complexities is essential for optimizing your code and making efficient choices when solving problems. Utilize profiling tools, measure execution times, and use appropriate data structures and algorithms to achieve the desired performance.

As an exercise, review the code in the python, section 2.4, and implement those scenarios in C++. Walk through the code to confirm the time and space complexities to make sure a thorough understanding. Understanding this section is crucial in writing effective and efficient code in all languages.

Chapter 4: Linear Data Structures

Linear data structures are the building blocks of more complex data structures and algorithms. In this chapter, we'll explore key linear data structures such as arrays, linked lists, stacks, and queues. You'll understand their characteristics, implementation, and when to use them in your Python and C++ projects.

4.1 Arrays and Linked Lists

Arrays and linked lists are fundamental data structures for organizing and storing collections of elements. In this section, we'll explore these data structures, their characteristics, and how to work with them effectively.

4.1.1 Understanding Arrays

An array is a fixed-size collection of elements, all of the same data type. Arrays provide efficient memory management as the elements are stored in contiguous memory locations, allowing for fast random access. However, arrays have a fixed size determined at compile time, which can limit their flexibility.

4.1.2 Defining and Accessing Arrays

In C++, you define an array by specifying its data type and size. For example, to create an array of integers with five elements:

```
1    int myArray[5];
```
Figure 4.1

Since arrays don't actually exist in Python but rather a 'list' which contains pointers to data. This allows python to contain all data types in one data structure.

```
1    myArray = []
2    myArray.append(5)
3    myArray.append('A')
```
Figure 4.2

In C++, you can access array elements using zero-based indexing, like this:

```
1    // Assign 42 to the first element
2    myArray[0] = 42;
3    // Retrieve the third element's value
4    int value = myArray[2];
```
Figure 4.3

In python you are also able to access elements using the square brackets '[]' as an accessor to a list with the index placed inside those brackets. Python is also 0-based, meaning we start from 0 instead of 1 for the first item.

4.1.3 Understanding Linked Lists

A linked list is a dynamic data structure in which elements, called nodes, are connected by pointers. Each node contains data and a reference to the next node in the list. Linked lists can grow or shrink dynamically during runtime, making them more flexible than arrays.

4.1.4 Defining and Using Linked Lists

In C++, you can create a linked list by defining a custom class for nodes and manipulating them through pointers:

```
1    class Node {
2    public:
3        int data;
4        Node* next;
5    };
6
7    Node* head = nullptr; // Initialize an empty linked list
```
Figure 4.4

You can insert, delete, and traverse nodes in the linked list using pointer manipulation:

```
1    Node* newNode = new Node();
2    newNode->data = 10;
3    newNode->next = head;
4    head = newNode; // Insert a new node at the beginning
5
6    Node* currentNode = head;
7    while (currentNode != nullptr) {
8        // Process currentNode
9        currentNode = currentNode->next;
10   }
```
Figure 4.5

The same can be done in Python as shown below. Be sure to try these implementations, as that is the best way to really understand their operations. There is no better way to understand a data structure than implementing one.

```
1    class Node:
2        def __init__(self, data):
3            self.data = data
4            self.next = None
5
6    class LinkedList:
7        def __init__(self):
8            self.head = None
9
10       def insert_at_beginning(self, data):
11           new_node = Node(data)
12           new_node.next = self.head
13           self.head = new_node
14
15       def traverse(self):
16           current_node = self.head
17           while current_node:
18               print(current_node.data)
19               current_node = current_node.next
20
21   # Create an empty linked list
22   my_linked_list = LinkedList()
23
24   # Insert nodes at the beginning
25   my_linked_list.insert_at_beginning(10)
26   my_linked_list.insert_at_beginning(20)
27   my_linked_list.insert_at_beginning(30)
28
29   # Traverse and print the linked list
30   my_linked_list.traverse()
```

Figure 4.6

4.1.5 Common Operations

Both arrays and linked lists support common operations such as accessing elements and iterating through the collection. However, arrays have a fixed size, and adding elements beyond that size can lead to undefined behavior. Linked lists, on the other hand, automatically manage their size, making them safer and more flexible.

4.1.6 Efficiency and Use Cases

Arrays offer efficient memory usage and fast random access. They are suitable for situations where a fixed-size collection is sufficient. Linked lists, with their dynamic sizing, are a more versatile choice when the number of elements can change during program execution. Linked lists may have a slight overhead due to pointer manipulation but provide ease of use and flexibility in return.

As we continue our exploration of data structures and algorithms, arrays and linked lists will be fundamental tools in your programming toolkit. You'll learn how to create, manipulate, and utilize these structures effectively, understanding when each is the best fit for the problem at hand. This knowledge will empower you to tackle a wide range of data processing tasks and algorithm implementations.

4.2 Stacks and Queues

Stacks and queues are essential data structures with specific behaviors and use cases. In this section, we'll explore their characteristics and how to implement and use them effectively.

4.2.1 Understanding Stacks

A stack is a linear data structure that follows the Last-In, First-Out (LIFO) principle. Think of it as a stack of books where the last book placed on top is the first one you pick up. In programming, a stack is a collection of elements with two primary operations: "push," which adds an element to the top, and "pop," which removes the top element. Stacks are used for tasks like tracking function calls, undo functionality in applications, and parsing expressions.

4.2.2 Defining and Using Stacks

In Python, you can implement a stack using a list:

```python
my_stack = []

# Push elements onto the stack
my_stack.append(10)
my_stack.append(20)
my_stack.append(30)

# Pop elements from the stack
top_element = my_stack.pop()  # Removes and returns 30
```

Figure 4.7

4.2.3 Understanding Queues

A queue is another linear data structure that adheres to the First-In, First-Out (FIFO) principle. Picture a queue of people waiting in line; the first person in line is the first to be served. In programming, a queue is a collection of elements with two primary operations: "enqueue," which adds an element to the back, and "dequeue," which removes the front element. Queues are used for tasks like managing tasks in a printer queue, scheduling processes in an operating system, and implementing breadth-first search algorithms.

4.2.4 Defining and Using Queues

In Python, you can implement a queue using the `collections.deque` class from the standard library:

```
1    from collections import deque
2
3    my_queue = deque()
4
5    # Enqueue elements
6    my_queue.append(10)
7    my_queue.append(20)
8    my_queue.append(30)
9
10   # Dequeue elements
11   front_element = my_queue.popleft()  # Removes and returns 10
```

Figure 4.8

4.2.5 Common Use Cases

Stacks and queues find applications in a wide array of scenarios.
Stacks are used for maintaining a history of actions, such as in web
browsers' back buttons. They're also employed in evaluating
mathematical expressions, where operators and operands are
arranged in postfix or prefix notations. Queues, on the other hand,
are vital for scheduling tasks and managing resources in a fair
manner. They ensure that the first task that arrives is the first one to
be processed, making them suitable for various algorithms and real-
world systems.

4.2.6 Efficiency and Data Structures

Efficiency considerations are vital when working with stacks and
queues. Stacks, as a basic structure, offer O(1) time complexity for
both push and pop operations. Queues also provide O(1) time
complexity for enqueue and dequeue operations. These data
structures are designed for fast access to the top element (stack) or
the front element (queue).

4.3 Implementation in Python and C++

Here is an example of how a stack can be implemented in Python.
While there are many libraries that provide these data structures or
built in data structures that can also be used as a stack, as shown
previously in section 4.2.2, the best way to learn and understand

39

how these data structures work is to implement one from scratch, and then see how you can modify and possible improve their function. This is also a great way to learn and see how you can modify data structures to a specific use case, which can be very common in practice, depending on role and job type.

```python
class Stack:
    def __init__(self):
        self.items = []

    def is_empty(self):
        return len(self.items) == 0

    def push(self, item):
        self.items.append(item)

    def pop(self):
        if not self.is_empty():
            return self.items.pop()
        else:
            return None

    def peek(self):
        if not self.is_empty():
            return self.items[-1]
        else:
            return None

    def size(self):
        return len(self.items)
```
Figure 4.9

The next example is the same thing but in C++. Building data structures to hold different types of data is very common in practice and is extremely useful when building anything from low-level drivers to GUI interfaces, delivering data to front end users.

40

```cpp
1    #include <iostream>
2    #include <vector>
3
4    class Stack {
5    private:
6        std::vector<int> items;
7
8    public:
9        bool is_empty() {
10           return items.empty();
11       }
12
13       void push(int item) {
14           items.push_back(item);
15       }
16
17       int pop() {
18           if (!is_empty()) {
19               int top = items.back();
20               items.pop_back();
21               return top;
22           } else {
23               return -1;
24           }
25       }
26
27       int peek() {
28           if (!is_empty()) {
29               return items.back();
30           } else {
31               return -1;
32           }
33       }
34
35       int size() {
36           return items.size();
37       }
38   };
```
Figure 4.10

The next two figures will show in both Python and C++ the implementation of a Queue using the deque class in both.

```python
from collections import deque

class Queue:
    def __init__(self):
        self.items = deque()

    def is_empty(self):
        return len(self.items) == 0

    def enqueue(self, item):
        self.items.append(item)

    def dequeue(self):
        if not self.is_empty():
            return self.items.popleft()
        else:
            return None

    def front(self):
        if not self.is_empty():
            return self.items[0]
        else:
            return None

    def size(self):
        return len(self.items)
```

Figure 4.11

```cpp
1    #include <iostream>
2    #include <deque>
3
4    class Queue {
5    private:
6        std::deque<int> items;
7
8    public:
9        bool is_empty() {
10           return items.empty();
11       }
12
13       void enqueue(int item) {
14           items.push_back(item);
15       }
16
17       int dequeue() {
18           if (!is_empty()) {
19               int front = items.front();
20               items.pop_front();
21               return front;
22           } else {
23               return -1;
24           }
25       }
26
27       int front() {
28           if (!is_empty()) {
29               return items.front();
30           } else {
31               return -1;
32           }
33       }
34
35       int size() {
36           return items.size();
37       }
38   };
```

Figure 4.12

43

Again, it is strongly encouraged to implement all these data structures and play around with them and really get to understand how they work. These will be the building blocks for many other implementations and understandings throughout an entire career.

4.4 Comparing Performance

When choosing data structures for your applications, it's important to consider the performance characteristics of each structure and select the one that best fits your specific use case. In this section, we'll compare the performance of various data structures to help you make informed decisions.

4.4.1 Array vs. Linked List

Access Time

- Arrays offer constant-time access to elements since they are stored in contiguous memory locations.
- Linked lists may require linear time for access, as you may need to traverse the list from the head to the desired element.

Insertion/Deletion Time

- Arrays may require shifting elements to accommodate insertions or deletions, leading to a time complexity of $O(n)$.
- Linked lists excel in insertion and deletion operations, typically requiring $O(1)$ time to insert or delete a node.

Memory Usage

- Arrays require memory for a fixed number of elements, leading to potential memory wastage if not fully utilized.
- Linked lists efficiently allocate memory as nodes are added, reducing memory wastage.

Stack vs. Queue

Stack (LIFO)

- Stacks are well-suited for situations where the most recent items are accessed frequently, such as function call management and undo operations.
- They offer O(1) time complexity for push and pop operations, making them efficient for these use cases.

Queue (FIFO)

- Queues are ideal for scenarios where the first-in, first-out order is essential, such as task scheduling and breadth-first search algorithms.
- They also offer O(1) time complexity for enqueue and dequeue operations, ensuring that the earliest elements are processed first.

4.4.2 Array vs. Dynamic Array (Vector)

Size Flexibility

- Arrays have a fixed size, determined at compile time, making them inflexible when the number of elements is unknown in advance.
- Dynamic arrays (vectors) can grow or shrink dynamically during runtime, making them a flexible choice when the size is variable.

Insertion/Deletion Time

- Arrays may require shifting elements for insertions or deletions, leading to O(n) time complexity.
- Dynamic arrays efficiently handle insertions and deletions, usually requiring amortized O(1) time for these operations.

Memory Usage

- Arrays allocate memory for a fixed number of elements, potentially causing memory wastage.
- Dynamic arrays allocate memory based on the current number of elements, reducing memory wastage.

4.4.3 Linked List vs. Dynamic Array (Vector)

Size Flexibility

- Linked lists can grow or shrink dynamically, making them suitable for scenarios with varying element counts.
- Dynamic arrays (vectors) also offer dynamic sizing, providing similar flexibility.

Access Time

- Linked lists may require linear time for access, as you may need to traverse the list from the head to the desired element.
- Dynamic arrays provide $O(1)$ time for access due to contiguous memory storage.

Insertion/Deletion Time

- Linked lists efficiently handle insertions and deletions, usually requiring $O(1)$ time for these operations.
- Dynamic arrays also handle insertions and deletions efficiently, typically requiring amortized $O(1)$ time.

4.4.4 Choosing the Right Data Structure

Performance considerations are essential when selecting a data structure. Choose the one that best matches the needs of your application.

Consider the specific operations your application requires and the frequency of those operations. For example, if you need to frequently insert or delete elements, a linked list may be more suitable. If you need fast random access, an array might be a better choice.

4.4.5 Real World Considerations

Keep in mind that real-world performance can be influenced by various factors, such as hardware, compiler optimizations, and specific use cases. Always consider the specific constraints and requirements of your project and be ready to adapt your choices accordingly.

In your journey to becoming a proficient programmer, understanding and comparing performance is a crucial skill. You'll learn to make informed decisions about data structures and algorithms, enabling you to tackle a wide range of data processing tasks and create efficient solutions for real-world problems.

Chapter 5: Non-Linear Data Structures

Non-linear data structures differ from linear structures like arrays and linked lists in that they allow elements to be organized in more complex relationships. In this section, we'll explore non-linear data structures, including trees and graphs, and discuss their characteristics and use cases. Following this chapter there will be dedicated chapters that go more in-depth on some of these data structures and the algorithms commonly used to traverse and interact with them.

5.1 Understanding Trees

Trees are hierarchical data structures consisting of nodes connected by edges. They have a single root node and can have zero or more child nodes. Each node in a tree may have a parent and zero or more children, creating a branching structure. Trees are used for tasks like representing hierarchical data, organizing information, and efficient searching and sorting.

5.1.1 Types of Trees

Binary Tree

A tree where each node has at most two children, known as the left child and the right child. Binary trees are used for binary search trees, expression trees, and more.

Binary Search Tree (BST)

A type of binary tree with the property that the left subtree of a node contains values less than the node's value, and the right subtree contains values greater. BSTs enable efficient searching, insertion, and deletion.

Balanced Tree

A binary tree where the left and right subtrees are balanced, ensuring that operations like searching and insertion have a logarithmic time complexity.

Red-Black Tree

A self-balancing binary search tree where nodes are colored red or black to maintain balance and ensure logarithmic time complexity for various operations.

5.2 Understanding Graphs

Graphs are collections of nodes connected by edges. Unlike trees, graphs do not have a fixed root node, and they can have cycles (closed loops). Graphs are used for modeling complex relationships, including social networks, transportation networks, and dependency networks in software.

5.2.1 Types of Graphs

Directed Graph (Digraph)

A graph where edges have a direction, going from one node to another. Directed graphs are used for modeling one-way relationships or processes.

Undirected Graph

A graph where edges have no direction, meaning they connect nodes bidirectionally. Undirected graphs are used for modeling symmetrical relationships.

Weighted Graph

A graph where edges have weights or costs associated with them. Weighted graphs are used for solving optimization problems, such as finding the shortest path in a network.

Cyclic Graph

A graph that contains at least one cycle (a closed loop). Cyclic graphs can represent scenarios with feedback loops or recurring processes.

5.3 Use Cases and Applications

- Trees are used for representing hierarchical data, organizing file systems, implementing data structures like AVL trees and B-trees, and enabling efficient searching and sorting.
- Graphs are employed in a wide range of applications, including social networks, recommendation systems, network routing, shortest path algorithms (e.g., Dijkstra's algorithm), and dependency resolution in software.

5.4 Complexity and Efficiency

- The time complexity of operations in trees and graphs can vary depending on the specific type and structure of the tree or graph. Balanced trees and efficient algorithms are often used to ensure logarithmic time complexity.
- The choice of the appropriate type of tree or graph depends on the problem's requirements. Trees are often used for hierarchical data, while graphs are used for modeling complex relationships.

Understanding and effectively using non-linear data structures like trees and graphs is essential for solving a wide range of problems in computer science and software engineering. These data structures provide the foundation for efficient search and organization, enabling the development of robust algorithms and applications.

5.5 Trees: Binary Trees, Binary Search Trees

Binary trees and binary search trees (BSTs) are fundamental non-linear data structures that play a crucial role in organizing and searching for data efficiently. In this section, we'll explore binary trees and BSTs, their characteristics, and how they are used in various applications.

5.5.1 Binary Trees

A binary tree is a hierarchical data structure that consists of nodes connected by edges. Each node has at most two children: a left child and a right child. Binary trees are used for organizing data hierarchically and efficiently. They provide a foundation for more complex structures like binary search trees.

5.5.2 Binary Search Trees (BSTs)

A binary search tree is a type of binary tree with the following properties:
- Each node has a value or key.
- The left subtree of a node contains values less than the node's key.
- The right subtree of a node contains values greater than the node's key.

BSTs enable efficient searching, insertion, and deletion operations. They provide an ordered structure that simplifies the process of finding, adding, and removing elements from the tree.

5.5.2.1 Operations on Binary Search Trees

Searching

To find a specific element in a BST, you can perform a search operation by comparing the target value with the values of nodes in the tree. BSTs have efficient average-case time complexity for searching, typically O(log n), where n is the number of nodes in the tree. In the worst case, when the tree is unbalanced, it can be O(n).

Insertion

To add a new element to a BST, you follow a set of rules for placement. Starting at the root node, you compare the new element with each node, moving left or right accordingly until you find an empty spot for insertion. The insertion operation also has an average-case time complexity of O(log n).

Deletion

Removing an element from a BST requires more care. If the node to delete has no children, it can be removed directly. If it has one child, the child takes its place. If it has two children, the tree's structure must be adjusted. Deleting a node in a BST also has an average-case time complexity of O(log n).

5.5.3 Balanced Binary Search Trees

Balanced binary search trees are structured to maintain balance in the tree, ensuring that the left and right subtrees are of approximately equal height. These trees, like AVL trees and Red-Black trees, guarantee that operations like searching, insertion, and deletion have a logarithmic time complexity.

5.5.3.1 Use Cases and Applications

Binary search trees are used for various applications, including:
- Storing and searching for data efficiently.

- Implementing data structures like sets and maps.
- Creating efficient ordered data structures for databases and file systems.
- Enabling fast searching and sorting algorithms.
- Providing a foundation for self-balancing trees like AVL and Red-Black trees.

Binary trees and binary search trees are foundational data structures that facilitate efficient data organization and retrieval. Understanding their properties and operations is essential for designing algorithms, data structures, and software applications where ordered data management is crucial.

5.5.4 Implementation of Binary Trees and BST's

Implementing binary trees and binary search trees (BSTs) involves creating the data structure and implementing various operations to manage the tree effectively. In this section, we'll explore how to implement binary trees and BSTs in Python and C++, along with the essential operations.

5.5.4.1 Implementing Binary Trees in Python

A binary tree can be implemented in Python using custom classes for nodes and, if needed, a class for the tree itself. Here's an example of a simple binary tree implementation:

```
1    class TreeNode:
2        def __init__(self, key):
3            self.key = key
4            self.left = None
5            self.right = None
6
7
8    # Creating a binary tree
9    root = TreeNode(10)
10   root.left = TreeNode(5)
11   root.right = TreeNode(15)
12   root.left.left = TreeNode(3)
13   root.left.right = TreeNode(7)
```

Figure 5.1

5.5.4.2 Implementing Binary Search Trees in Python

A binary search tree (BST) can be implemented by extending the binary tree implementation and ensuring the properties of BST are maintained during insertion and deletion. Here's a basic example of a BST implementation in Python:

54

```python
1   class TreeNode:
2       def __init__(self, key):
3           self.key = key
4           self.left = None
5           self.right = None
6
7
8   class BinarySearchTree:
9       def __init__(self):
10          self.root = None
11
12      def insert(self, key):
13          self.root = self._insert(self.root, key)
14
15      def _insert(self, root, key):
16          if not root:
17              return TreeNode(key)
18          if key < root.key:
19              root.left = self._insert(root.left, key)
20          elif key > root.key:
21              root.right = self._insert(root.right, key)
22          return root
```

Figure 5.2

5.5.4.3 Implementing Binary Trees in C++

In C++, binary trees can be implemented similarly, using custom classes for nodes and, if needed, a class for the tree itself. Here's an example of a simple binary tree implementation:

55

```
1    #include <iostream>
2
3    class TreeNode {
4    public:
5        int key;
6        TreeNode* left;
7        TreeNode* right;
8
9        TreeNode(int key) : key(key), left(nullptr), right(nullptr) {}
10   };
11
12   // Creating a binary tree
13   TreeNode* root = new TreeNode(10);
14   root->left = new TreeNode(5);
15   root->right = new TreeNode(15);
16   root->left->left = new TreeNode(3);
17   root->left->right = new TreeNode(7);
```

Figure 5.3

5.5.4.4 Implementing Binary Search Trees in C++

A binary search tree (BST) in C++ can be implemented by
extending the binary tree implementation and ensuring that the
properties of BST are maintained during insertion and deletion.
Here's a basic example of a BST implementation in C++:

56

```cpp
1    #include <iostream>
2
3    class TreeNode {
4    public:
5        int key;
6        TreeNode* left;
7        TreeNode* right;
8
9        TreeNode(int key) : key(key), left(nullptr), right(nullptr) {}
10   };
11
12   class BinarySearchTree {
13   public:
14       TreeNode* root;
15
16       BinarySearchTree() : root(nullptr) {}
17
18       void insert(int key) {
19           root = _insert(root, key);
20       }
21
22       TreeNode* _insert(TreeNode* root, int key) {
23           if (!root) {
24               return new TreeNode(key);
25           }
26           if (key < root->key) {
27               root->left = _insert(root->left, key);
28           } else if (key > root->key) {
29               root->right = _insert(root->right, key);
30           }
31           return root;
32       }
33   };
```

Figure 5.4

These are basic examples of binary tree and BST implementations in Python and C++. Implementations can be extended to include other operations like searching, deletion, and traversal. Understanding the inner workings of these data structures and how to implement them is crucial for building more complex data structures and algorithms in your software applications.

57

5.6 Heaps and Priority Queues

Heaps and priority queues are versatile data structures used for managing and retrieving elements based on their priority. In this section, we'll explore heaps and priority queues, their characteristics, and how they are used in various applications.

5.6.1 Understanding Heaps

A heap is a specialized tree-based data structure that satisfies the heap property. In a max-heap, for any given node C, the value of C is greater than or equal to the values of its children. In a min-heap, it is the opposite, where the value of C is less than or equal to the values of its children. Heaps are used for efficient selection of extreme values and are at the core of priority queues.

5.6.2 Types of Heaps

Max-Heap

In a max-heap, the maximum value is at the root, and each parent node has a value greater than or equal to its children's values. Max-heaps are used for implementing priority queues, where the highest-priority item is always at the front.

Min-Heap

In a min-heap, the minimum value is at the root, and each parent node has a value less than or equal to its children's values. Min-heaps are used for tasks like scheduling processes with the shortest time remaining.

5.6.3 Operations on Heaps

Insertion

To insert an element into a heap, you add it to the next available position and then sift it up (for max-heaps) or sift it down (for min-heaps) to maintain the heap property. The time complexity of insertion is O(log n), where n is the number of elements in the heap.

Extraction

To retrieve the extreme value (the maximum in a max-heap or the minimum in a min-heap), you remove the root element and replace it with the last element. Afterward, you sift this element down (for max-heaps) or sift it up (for min-heaps). The time complexity of extraction is O(log n).

5.6.4 Understanding Priority Queues

A priority queue is an abstract data type that supports operations like insertion and extraction of elements with priorities. Priority queues can be implemented using heaps, providing efficient management of items based on their priorities.

5.6.5 Use Cases and Applications

Priority queues are used in various applications, including:
- Task scheduling in operating systems.
- Pathfinding algorithms (e.g., Dijkstra's algorithm and A* search).
- Huffman coding for data compression.
- Event-driven simulations.
- Implementing efficient algorithms for sorting and graph algorithms.

5.6.6 Complexity and Efficiency

- Heaps and priority queues offer efficient access to the extreme values, making them ideal for tasks where such values need to be quickly identified.
- The time complexity of insertion and extraction operations in heaps is O(log n), making them efficient for maintaining ordered collections.

5.6.7 Implementation of a Max Heap and Priority Queue

Implementing a max heap and a priority queue involves creating the data structure and implementing key operations to maintain the heap property and prioritize elements effectively. In this section, we'll explore how to implement a max heap and a priority queue in Python and C++, along with essential operations.

5.6.7.1 Implementing a Max Heap in Python

A max heap can be implemented in Python using a list or array, with custom functions to maintain the heap property. Here's a basic example:

```
1    class MaxHeap:
2        def __init__(self):
3            self.heap = []
4
5        def insert(self, item):
6            self.heap.append(item)
7            self._heapify_up()
8
9        def extract_max(self):
10           if len(self.heap) == 0:
11               return None
12
13           if len(self.heap) == 1:
14               return self.heap.pop()
15
16           max_val = self.heap[0]
17           self.heap[0] = self.heap.pop()
18           self._heapify_down()
19
20           return max_val
21
22       def _heapify_up(self):
23           index = len(self.heap) - 1
24           while index > 0:
25               parent_index = (index - 1) // 2
26               if self.heap[index] > self.heap[parent_index]:
27                   self.heap[index], self.heap[parent_index] \
28                       = self.heap[parent_index], self.heap[index]
29                   index = parent_index
30               else:
31                   break
32
```

Figure 5.5

```
33    def _heapify_down(self):
34        index = 0
35        while index < len(self.heap):
36            left_child_index = 2 * index + 1
37            right_child_index = 2 * index + 2
38            largest = index
39
40            if (
41                left_child_index < len(self.heap)
42                and self.heap[left_child_index] > self.heap[largest]
43            ):
44                largest = left_child_index
45
46            if (
47                right_child_index < len(self.heap)
48                and self.heap[right_child_index] > self.heap[largest]
49            ):
50                largest = right_child_index
51
52            if largest != index:
53                self.heap[index], self.heap[largest] \
54                    = self.heap[largest], self.heap[index]
55                index = largest
56            else:
57                break
58
```

Figure 5.6

5.6.7.2 Implementing a Max Heap in C++

In C++, a max heap can be implemented similarly using an array. Here's an example of a max heap implementation in C++:

```cpp
#include <iostream>
#include <vector>

class MaxHeap {
private:
    std::vector<int> heap;

    void heapify_up() {
        int index = heap.size() - 1;
        while (index > 0) {
            int parent_index = (index - 1) / 2;
            if (heap[index] > heap[parent_index]) {
                std::swap(heap[index], heap[parent_index]);
                index = parent_index;
            } else {
                break;
            }
        }
    }

    void heapify_down() {
        int index = 0;
        while (index < heap.size()) {
            int left_child_index = 2 * index + 1;
            int right_child_index = 2 * index + 2;
            int largest = index;

            if (left_child_index < heap.size()
                && heap[left_child_index] > heap[largest]) {
                largest = left_child_index;
            }

            if (right_child_index < heap.size()
                && heap[right_child_index] > heap[largest]) {
                largest = right_child_index;
            }

            if (largest != index) {
                std::swap(heap[index], heap[largest]);
                index = largest;
            } else {
                break;
            }
        }
    }
}
```

Figure 5.7

63

```
47    public:
48        void insert(int item) {
49            heap.push_back(item);
50            heapify_up();
51        }
52
53        int extract_max() {
54            if (heap.empty()) {
55                return -1;
56            }
57
58            if (heap.size() == 1) {
59                int max_val = heap[0];
60                heap.pop_back();
61                return max_val;
62            }
63
64            int max_val = heap[0];
65            heap[0] = heap.back();
66            heap.pop_back();
67            heapify_down();
68            return max_val;
69        }
70    };
71
72    int main() {
73        MaxHeap max_heap;
74        max_heap.insert(10);
75        max_heap.insert(20);
76        max_heap.insert(15);
77        max_heap.insert(30);
78        max_heap.insert(5);
79
80        std::cout << max_heap.extract_max() << std::endl;
81        // Output: 30
82        return 0;
83    }
```

Figure 5.8

5.6.7.3 Implementing a Priority Queue using a Max Heap

A priority queue can be implemented using a max heap, as elements with higher priorities are retrieved first. Here's a basic example of implementing a priority queue using a max heap in Python:

```python
1  class PriorityQueue:
2      def __init__(self):
3          self.max_heap = MaxHeap()
4
5      def insert(self, item, priority):
6          self.max_heap.insert((item, priority))
7
8      def extract_max(self):
9          return self.max_heap.extract_max()[0]
```

Figure 5.9

This implementation uses a tuple to associate items with their priorities. You can modify the implementation to use a custom class or struct for items with associated priorities in C++.

These implementations provide a foundation for working with max heaps and priority queues. You can extend them to include additional operations and adapt them to your specific needs for managing and prioritizing elements in your applications.

Understanding and effectively using heaps and priority queues is essential for solving problems where elements need to be organized by priority. These data structures provide a powerful tool for managing tasks, optimizing algorithms, and efficiently retrieving important information based on their significance.

As an exercise, try to implement a Priority Queue as done with Python but in C++.

5.7 Hash Tables

Hash tables, also known as hash maps, are essential data structures used for efficient data retrieval and storage. In this section, we'll explore hash tables, their characteristics, and provide examples of implementation in both Python and C++.

5.7.1 Understanding Hash Tables

A hash table is a data structure that stores key-value pairs and enables fast data retrieval based on the key. It uses a hash function to map the key to an index in an array, allowing for direct access to the associated value. Hash tables provide constant-time ($O(1)$) average-case time complexity for insertion, retrieval, and deletion.

5.7.2 Components of a Hash Table

1. Array An array is the underlying data structure used to store key-value pairs.
2. Hash Function A hash function takes a key and computes an index in the array where the associated value will be stored.
3. Collision Resolution Since multiple keys can map to the same index (a collision), collision resolution strategies are used to handle collisions and ensure that all keys can be retrieved correctly.

5.7.3 Hash Function and Collision Resolution

- A good hash function uniformly distributes keys across the array to minimize collisions.
- Collision resolution methods include chaining (using linked lists to store multiple values at the same index) and open addressing (searching for the next available slot in the array).

5.7.4 Implementing a Hash Table in Python

Here's a basic example of implementing a hash table in Python using dictionaries, which are a built-in implementation of a hash table:

```python
class HashTable:
    def __init__(self, size):
        self.size = size
        self.table = [None] * size

    def _hash(self, key):
        return hash(key) % self.size

    def insert(self, key, value):
        index = self._hash(key)
        if self.table[index] is None:
            self.table[index] = []
        self.table[index].append((key, value))

    def search(self, key):
        index = self._hash(key)
        if self.table[index] is not None:
            for k, v in self.table[index]:
                if k == key:
                    return v
        return None
```

Figure 5.10

5.7.5 Implementing a Hash Table in C++

In C++, you can implement a hash table using arrays and linked lists. Here's an example:

```cpp
1   #include <iostream>
2   #include <list>
3   #include <vector>
4
5   class HashTable {
6   private:
7       int size;
8       std::vector<std::list<std::pair<int, int>>> table;
9
10      int hash(int key) {
11          return key % size;
12      }
13
14  public:
15      HashTable(int table_size) : size(table_size), table(table_size) {}
16
17      void insert(int key, int value) {
18          int index = hash(key);
19          for (auto& pair : table[index]) {
20              if (pair.first == key) {
21                  pair.second = value;
22                  return;
23              }
24          }
25          table[index].emplace_back(key, value);
26      }
27
28      int search(int key) {
29          int index = hash(key);
30          for (const auto& pair : table[index]) {
31              if (pair.first == key) {
32                  return pair.second;
33              }
34          }
35          return -1;
36      }
37  };
38
39  int main() {
40      HashTable hash_table(10);
41      hash_table.insert(1, 42);
42      hash_table.insert(5, 17);
43      std::cout << hash_table.search(1) << std::endl; // Output: 42
44      return 0;
45  }
```

Figure 5.11

These examples provide a foundation for understanding and
implementing hash tables in both Python and C++. Hash tables are

versatile data structures used in various applications, such as implementing dictionaries, caches, and databases, and for optimizing data retrieval tasks.

Chapter 6: Advanced Data Structures

In this chapter, we'll take a look at advanced data structures that offer specialized and efficient solutions to complex problems. We'll explore graphs and various specialized data structures like tries, suffix trees, Fenwick trees, and segment trees. You'll learn how to implement these structures in Python and C++ and understand their unique applications.

6.1 Graphs and Graph Algorithms

Graphs are fundamental data structures used to represent complex relationships and solve a wide range of problems in computer science and beyond. In this section, we'll explore graphs, their characteristics, and key graph algorithms that help address various challenges.

6.1.1 Understanding Graphs

A graph is a collection of nodes (vertices) and edges that connect these nodes. Each edge may have a weight or cost associated with it, depending on the application. Graphs are versatile data structures that can represent diverse relationships, including social networks, transportation systems, dependency networks, and more.

6.1.2 Types of Graphs

i. Undirected Graphs In undirected graphs, edges have no direction, and the relationship between nodes is symmetric. If there is an edge from node A to node B, there is also an edge from node B to node A.

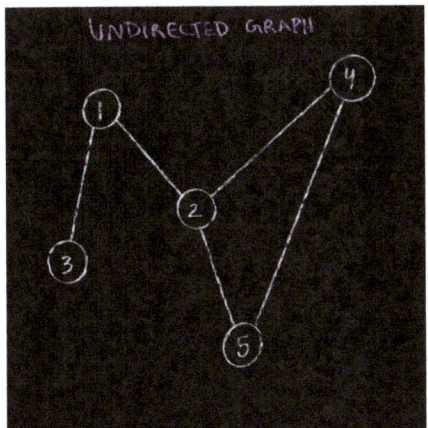

Figure 6.1

ii. Directed Graphs (Digraphs) In directed graphs, edges have a direction, and the relationship between nodes is asymmetric. Edges go from one node to another, but not necessarily in the reverse direction.

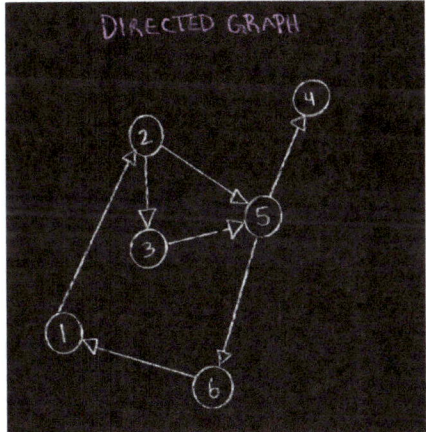

Figure 6.2

iii.   Weighted Graphs Weighted graphs assign a weight or cost to each edge, representing some measure of distance, cost, or importance.

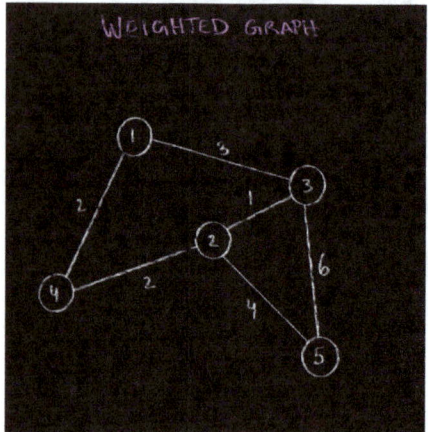

Figure 6.3

iv.   Cyclic and Acyclic Graphs A graph with at least one cycle (a closed loop) is cyclic, while one without any cycles is acyclic. Trees are a specific type of acyclic graph.

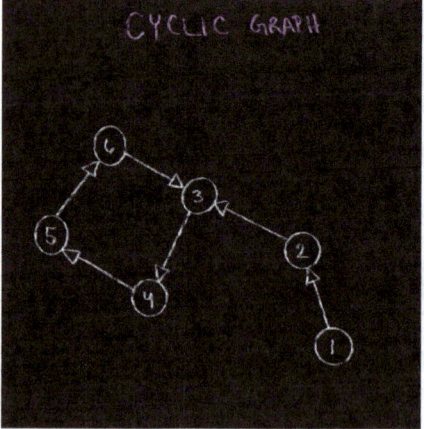

Figure 6.4

     72

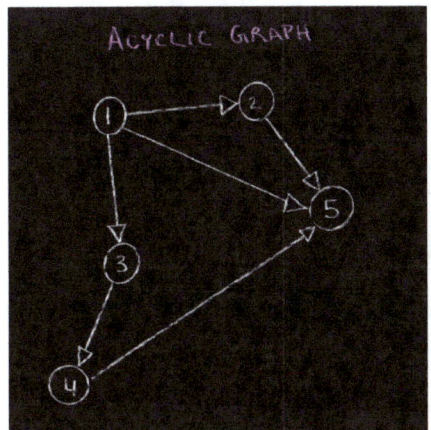

Figure 6.5

v. Connected Graphs A graph is connected if there is a path between any pair of nodes. In disconnected graphs, some nodes or components are not reachable from others.

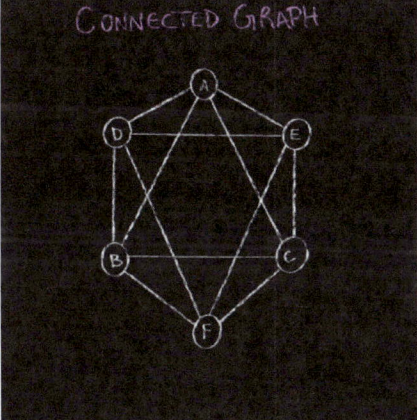

Figure 6.6

vi.   Sparse and Dense Graphs Sparse graphs have relatively few edges compared to the number of nodes, while dense graphs have many edges.

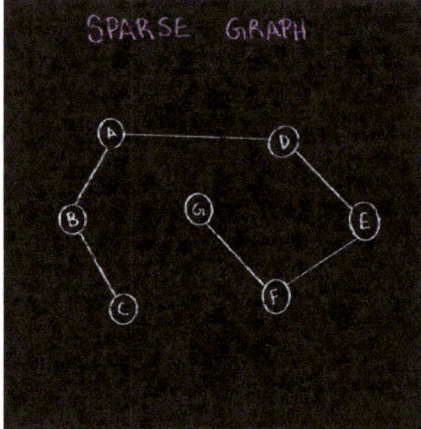

Figure 6.7

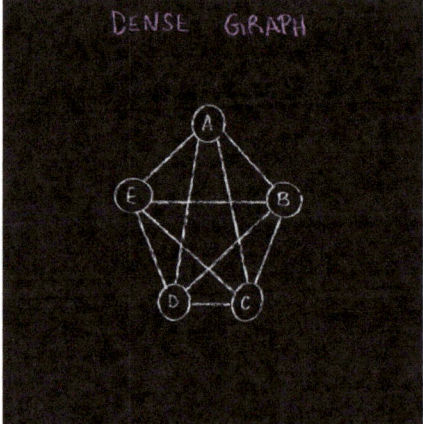

Figure 6.8

74

6.1.3 Graph Algorithms

Several important algorithms are used to analyze and manipulate graphs. Here are a few key graph algorithms:

6.1.3.1 Breadth-First Search (BFS)

BFS explores a graph level by level, starting from a source node. It's useful for finding the shortest path in unweighted graphs and exploring nearby nodes in a systematic manner.

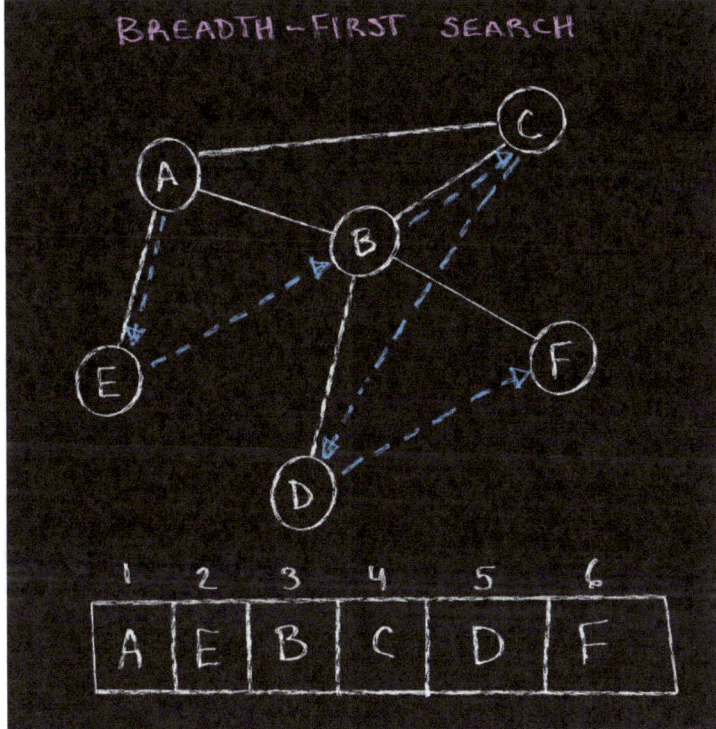

Figure 6.9

6.1.3.2 Depth-First Search (DFS)

DFS explores a graph by traversing as far as possible along each branch before backtracking. It's used in tasks like topological sorting, cycle detection, and connected components.

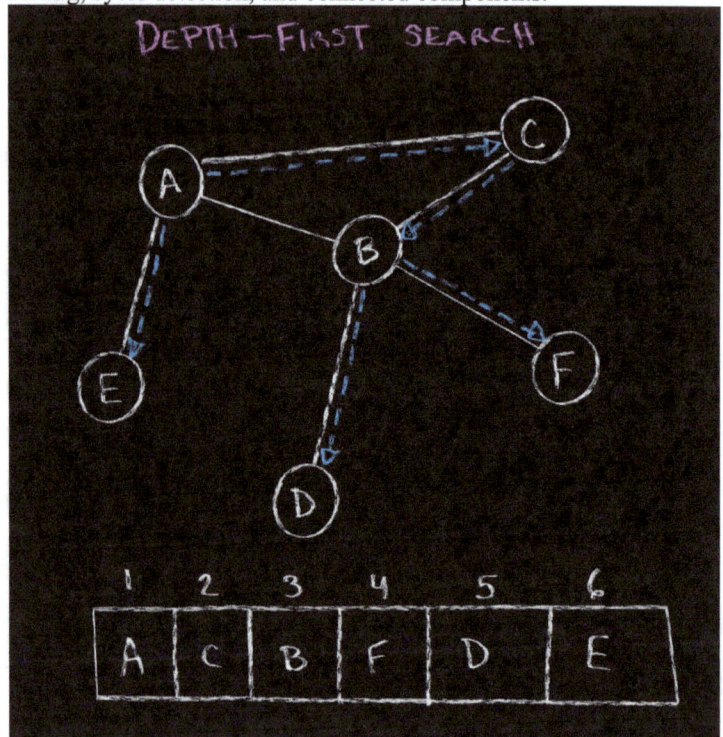

Figure 6.10

6.1.3.3 Dijkstra's Algorithm

Dijkstra's algorithm finds the shortest path from a source node to all other nodes in a weighted graph. It's widely used in applications such as navigation and network routing.

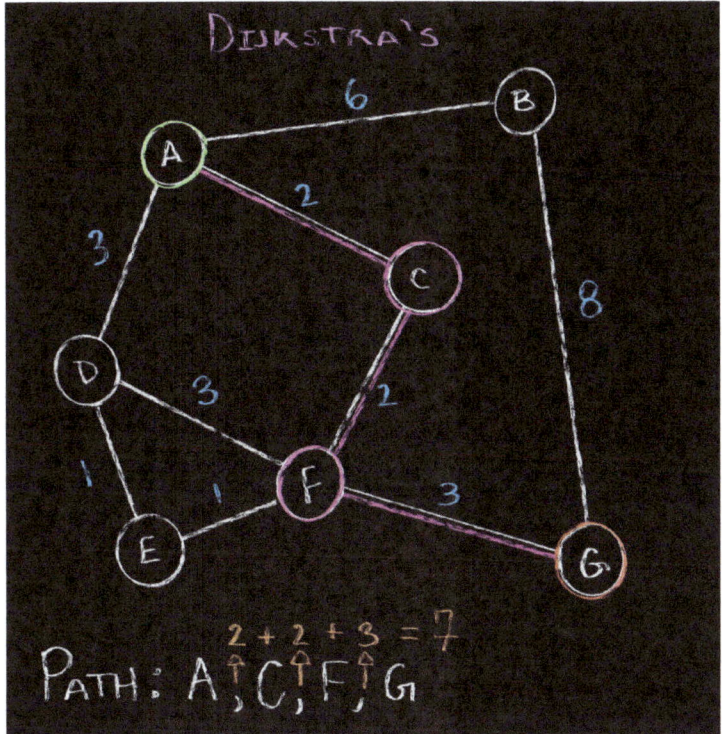

Figure 6.11

function Dijkstra(graph, source):
    create a set S to keep track of visited nodes
    create a list dist[] to store the shortest distance from the source to each node
    initialize dist[] with infinity for all nodes except the source, which is set to 0
    create a priority queue (min-heap) Q to store nodes with their tentative distances

    while Q is not empty:
        node = node with the smallest distance from Q
        add node to set S

        for each neighbor of node:
            if neighbor is not in S:
                calculate tentative distance to neighbor through the current node
                if the tentative distance is less than the stored distance for neighbor:
                    update the distance of neighbor in dist[]
                    add neighbor to Q with the new tentative distance

77

```
return dist
```

In this pseudo-code

graph represents the weighted graph with nodes and edges.
source is the starting node from which you want to find the shortest
paths to all other nodes.
S is a set that keeps track of visited nodes.
dist[] is an array that stores the shortest distances from the source to
all nodes. It is initialized with infinity for all nodes except the
source, which starts with a distance of 0.
Q is a priority queue (min-heap) used to select the node with the
smallest tentative distance in each iteration.
The algorithm proceeds by iteratively selecting the node with the
smallest distance from Q, marking it as visited by adding it to set **S**,
and updating the distances to its neighbors. This process continues
until all nodes have been visited, and dist contains the shortest
distances from the source to all nodes.
Note that the actual implementation of Dijkstra's Algorithm may
vary depending on the programming language and data structures
used, but this pseudo-code provides a high-level representation of
the algorithm's key steps.

6.1.3.4 Bellman-Ford Algorithm

The Bellman-Ford algorithm is used to find the shortest paths in
weighted graphs, including graphs with negative-weight edges. It
can handle graphs with negative cycles, but it may not provide the
optimal solution in such cases.

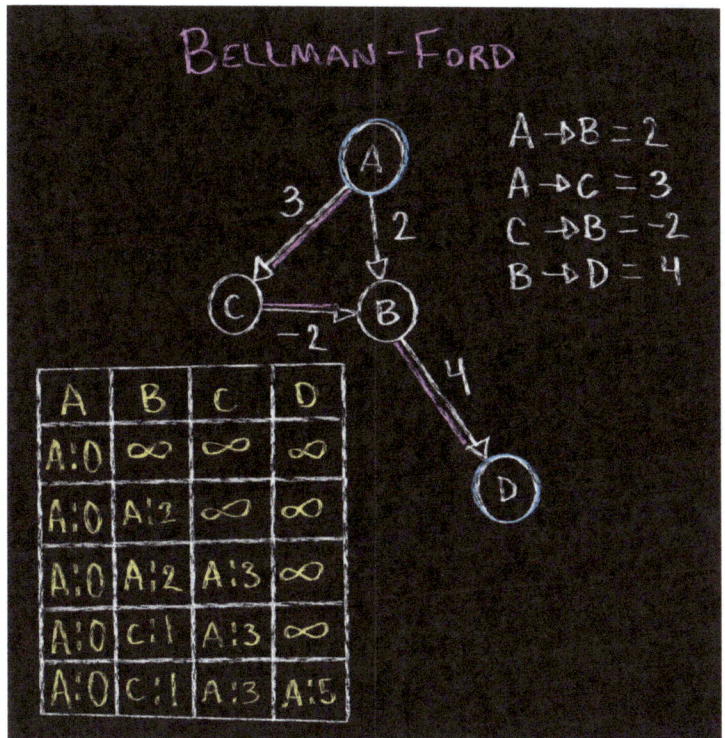

Figure 6.12

function BellmanFord(graph, source):
    create a list dist[] to store the shortest distance from the source to each node
    initialize dist[] with infinity for all nodes except the source, which is set to 0

    repeat (|V| - 1) times, where |V| is the number of nodes:
        for each edge (u, v) with weight w in the graph:
            if dist[u] + w < dist[v]:
                update dist[v] to dist[u] + w

    for each edge (u, v) with weight w in the graph:
        if dist[u] + w < dist[v]:
            return "Graph contains a negative-weight cycle"

    return dist

In this pseudo-code

graph represents the weighted graph with nodes and edges.
source is the starting node from which you want to find the shortest paths to all other nodes.
dist[] is an array that stores the shortest distances from the source to all nodes. It is initialized with infinity for all nodes except the source, which starts with a distance of 0.

The algorithm proceeds by iterating through all edges multiple times, relaxing (updating) the distance to each node if a shorter path is found. It repeats this process $|V|$ - 1 times, where $|V|$ is the number of nodes in the graph, to ensure convergence. After these iterations, if a shorter path is still found, it indicates the presence of a negative-weight cycle.

Bellman-Ford is a versatile algorithm, and its pseudo-code provides a high-level representation of its key steps. It is essential for finding shortest paths in graphs with negative-weight edges and is often used in applications like network routing and path optimization.

6.1.3.5 Floyd-Warshall Algorithm

The Floyd-Warshall algorithm computes the shortest paths between all pairs of nodes in a weighted graph, making it suitable for dense graphs. It can handle graphs with negative-weight edges but not negative cycles.

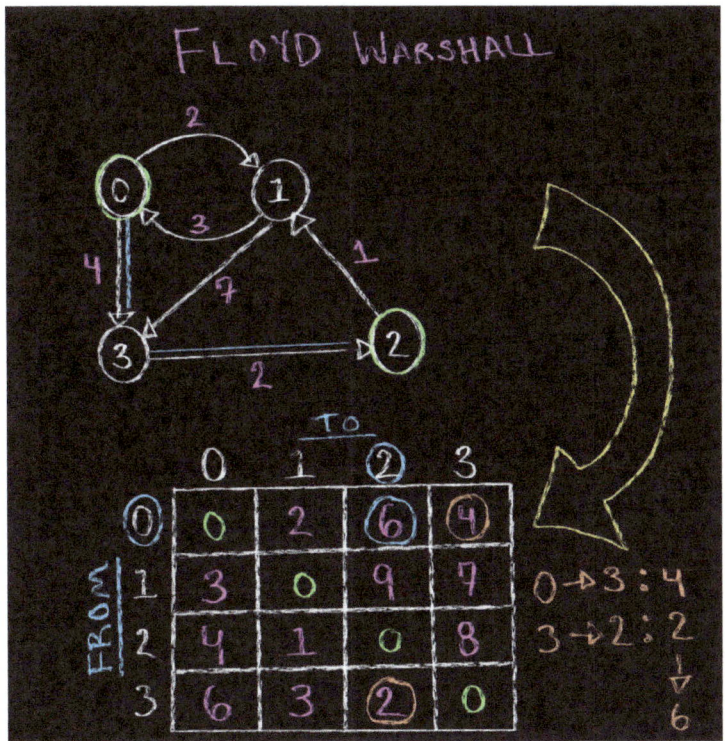

Figure 6.13

```
function FloydWarshall(graph):
    create a 2D array dist of size |V| x |V| and initialize it with infinity

    for each node u in graph:
        dist[u][u] = 0  // Distance from a node to itself is zero

    for each edge (u, v) with weight w in graph:
        dist[u][v] = w  // Set initial distance to the edge weight

    for each node k in graph:
        for each node i in graph:
            for each node j in graph:
                if dist[i][j] > dist[i][k] + dist[k][j]:
                    dist[i][j] = dist[i][k] + dist[k][j]

    return dist
```

In this pseudo-code

graph represents the weighted graph with nodes and edges.
dist is a 2D array of size $|V|$ x $|V|$, where $|V|$ is the number of nodes
in the graph, used to store the shortest distances between all pairs of
nodes. It is initialized with infinity for all pairs of nodes, except
when nodes are the same (diagonal), where the distance is set to
zero.

The algorithm uses three nested loops to iterate through all nodes
and compute the shortest paths. It repeatedly checks whether there is
a shorter path from node i to node j through an intermediate node k.
If such a path exists, it updates the distance accordingly.

The Floyd-Warshall Algorithm is a powerful tool for finding the
shortest paths between all pairs of nodes in a graph. It's commonly
used in applications like network routing and can be applied to both
dense and sparse graphs.

6.1.3.6 Kruskal's Algorithm

Kruskal's algorithm finds the minimum spanning tree of a graph,
which is a tree that spans all nodes with the minimum possible total
edge weight. It's used in network design and optimization.

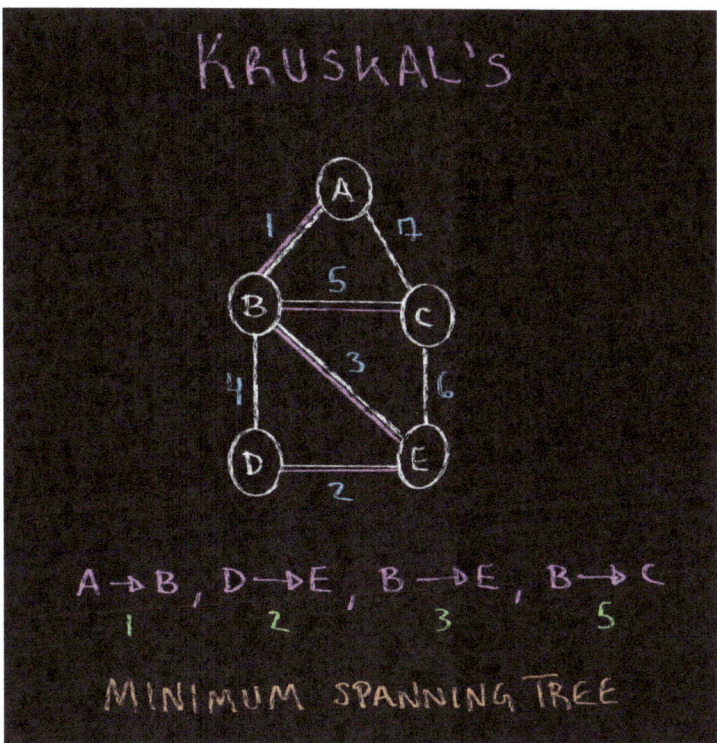

Figure 6.14

```
function Kruskal(graph):
    create a set of trees F, initially empty
    create a list of edges E, sorted by non-decreasing weight
    create an empty minimum spanning tree T

    for each node v in graph:
        create a tree containing only node v and add it to F

    while F has more than one tree:
        select and remove the minimum-weight edge (u, v) from E
        find the trees containing nodes u and v in F
        if the trees are in different sets:
            add edge (u, v) to T
            merge the two trees into a single tree and remove them from F

    return T
```

In this pseudo-code

graph represents the weighted graph with nodes and edges.
F is a set of trees representing the connected components of the
graph, initially created for each node.
E is a list of edges sorted by their weights in non-decreasing order.
T is the minimum spanning tree that Kruskal's Algorithm constructs.

The algorithm starts with each node in its own tree and iteratively
selects the minimum-weight edge from the sorted list E. If the nodes
connected by the edge belong to different trees in the set F, the edge
is added to the minimum spanning tree T, and the two trees are
merged into one. This process continues until there is only one tree
left in F.

Kruskal's Algorithm is a widely used algorithm for finding
minimum spanning trees in various applications, such as network
design and optimization, and it ensures that the minimum spanning
tree spans all nodes with the least total edge weight.

6.1.3.7 Prim's Algorithm

Prim's algorithm also finds the minimum spanning tree but starts
with a single node and grows the tree from there. It's used in similar
applications as Kruskal's algorithm.

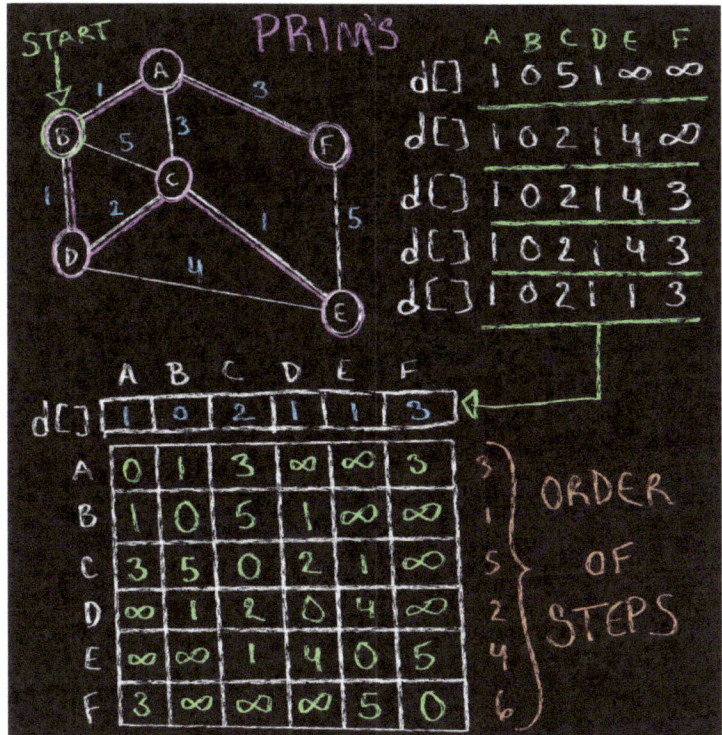

Figure 6.15

```
function Prim(graph):
    create a set of nodes V, initially empty
    create an empty minimum spanning tree T
    choose a starting node s
    add node s to V

    while V does not contain all nodes in the graph:
        find the minimum-weight edge (u, v) such that u is in V and v is not in V
        add edge (u, v) to T
        add node v to V

    return T
```

graph represents the weighted graph with nodes and edges.
V is a set of nodes, initially empty, representing the nodes included in the minimum spanning tree.
T is the minimum spanning tree that Prim's Algorithm constructs.

The algorithm starts with a chosen starting node s (can be any node in the graph) and adds it to the set V.

It then iteratively selects the minimum-weight edge that connects a node in V to a node not in V, adds the edge to the minimum spanning tree T, and adds the newly connected node to V. This process continues until all nodes are included in V.

Prim's Algorithm is another widely used algorithm for finding minimum spanning trees and has applications in network design and optimization. It ensures that the minimum spanning tree spans all nodes with the least total edge weight, similar to Kruskal's Algorithm.

6.1.3.8 A* Search Algorithm

A* is an informed search algorithm used for finding the shortest path in graphs, considering both the cost to reach a node and an estimate of the remaining cost to reach the goal. It's commonly used in pathfinding and route planning.

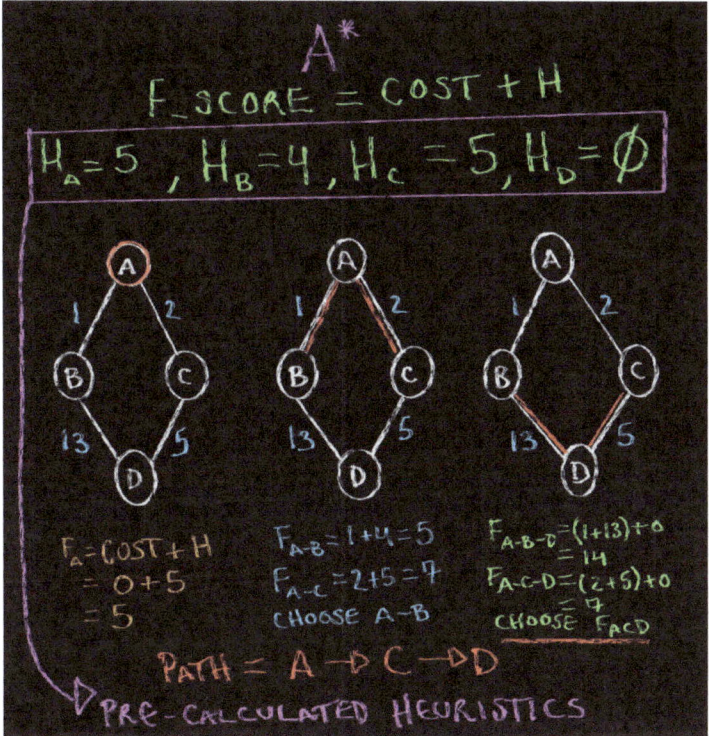

Figure 6.16

```
function AStar(graph, start, goal):
    create an open list of nodes, initially containing only the start node
    create a closed list of nodes, initially empty
    create a dictionary to store the cost from the start node to each node, initially with
infinity for all nodes except start (cost[start] = 0)
    create a dictionary to store the total estimated cost for each node (f_score), initially
with infinity for all nodes (f_score[start] = h(start, goal))

    while the open list is not empty:
        current = node in the open list with the lowest f_score
        if current is the goal node:
            return reconstruct_path(current)

        move current from the open list to the closed list

        for each neighbor in the neighbors of current:
```

```
tentative_g_score = cost[current] + cost(current, neighbor)
if tentative_g_score < cost[neighbor]:
    update cost[neighbor] to tentative_g_score
    update f_score[neighbor] to tentative_g_score + h(neighbor, goal)
    if neighbor is not in the open list:
        add neighbor to the open list

return "No path found"

function reconstruct_path(current):
    create a path list containing only the current node
    while current has a parent node:
        prepend current's parent node to the path
        current = current's parent node
    return the path
```

In this pseudo-code

graph represents the graph with nodes and edges.
start is the starting node.
goal is the destination node.

The algorithm maintains an open list of nodes to be evaluated and a closed list of nodes already evaluated.
cost is a dictionary storing the cost to reach each node from the start node.

f_score is a dictionary storing the total estimated cost (f-score) for each node, which is the sum of the cost to reach the node and an estimate of the remaining cost to reach the goal.

The algorithm iteratively selects the node with the lowest f-score from the open list, evaluates its neighbors, updates their costs and f-scores if a shorter path is found, and adds them to the open list if they are not there already. The process continues until the goal node is reached, and the path is reconstructed.

A* is widely used in pathfinding, route planning, and navigation systems, where it takes into account both the actual cost incurred so far and an estimate of the remaining cost to find an efficient path from a start node to a goal node.

Graphs and graph algorithms are essential tools for modeling and solving various real-world problems. These algorithms are widely used in areas like network design, computer graphics, recommendation systems, and more. By understanding the fundamentals of graphs and mastering key graph algorithms, you can become a more effective problem solver in the world of computer science and beyond.

6.2 Trie and Suffix Tree

Trie and Suffix Tree are specialized data structures primarily used for handling strings efficiently. In this section, we'll explore Trie and Suffix Tree, their characteristics, and their applications.

6.2.1 Understanding Trie

A Trie (pronounced "try") is a tree-like data structure that is used for efficient retrieval of strings. It's particularly useful for searching and storing dictionaries and text-based data. Each node in a Trie represents a character or part of a string, and the path from the root to a node forms a string. Tries have applications in spell checkers, autocomplete systems, and more.

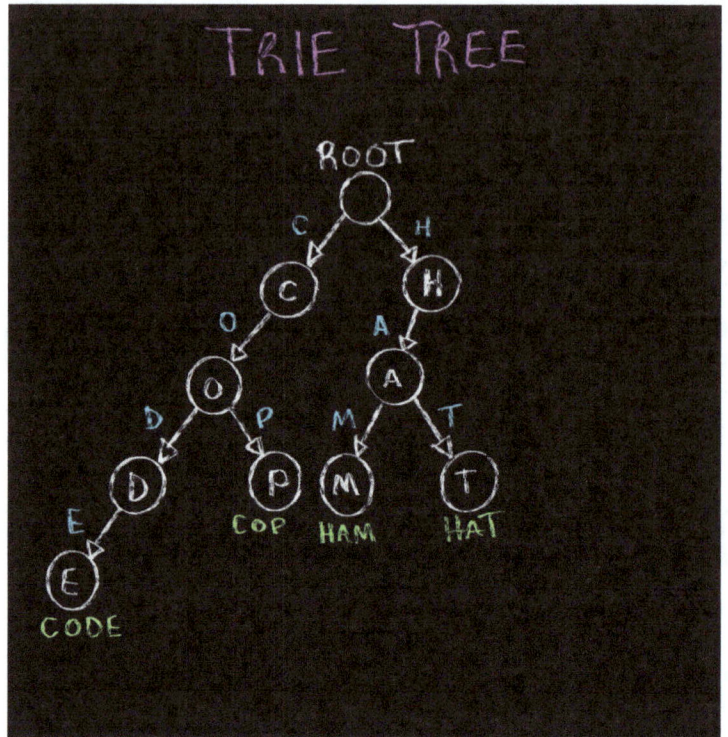

Figure 6.17

6.2.2 Key Components of a Trie

1. Root The starting point of the Trie.

2. Node Each node in the Trie represents a character and may have child nodes.

3. Edge The connection between a parent node and its child node represents a character.

4. Leaf Node A node that marks the end of a valid word or string.

90

6.2.3 Building a Trie

To build a Trie, insert each word or string character by character, starting from the root. If a character doesn't exist in the current path, create a new node and connect it to the parent node.

6.2.4 Searching in a Trie

Searching in a Trie involves traversing the tree from the root, one character at a time, until you reach the end of the input string. If the path exists in the Trie and ends in a leaf node, the string is found.

6.2.5 Understanding Suffix Tree

A Suffix Tree is an advanced data structure that represents all the suffixes of a given string in a compressed form. It's used for various string processing tasks, including substring searching, longest common substring, and pattern matching. Suffix Trees are highly efficient and compact, making them suitable for large text datasets.

Figure 6.18

6.2.6 Key Components of a Suffix Tree

1. Root The root of the Suffix Tree, representing an empty string.
2. Edge The edge connecting two nodes represents a character or a substring.
3. Internal Node Represents a non-empty substring.
4. Leaf Node Represents a suffix of the original string.

6.2.7 Building a Suffix Tree

Constructing a Suffix Tree involves repeatedly adding suffixes of the string to the tree. This process can be done efficiently using various algorithms, such as Ukkonen's algorithm.

6.2.8 Searching in a Suffix Tree

Suffix Trees enable fast substring and pattern searches by traversing the tree from the root, matching characters along the way, and stopping when the search string is exhausted or no further path is available.

6.2.9 Applications

- Tries are widely used in natural language processing, spell checkers, and autocomplete systems.
- Suffix Trees are used in string matching, DNA sequence analysis, and text indexing.

6.2.10 Conclusion

Trie and Suffix Tree are specialized data structures that excel in handling strings efficiently. Tries are valuable for string-based operations and are commonly used in various text processing applications. Suffix Trees, on the other hand, are powerful tools for substring and pattern matching and are indispensable in bioinformatics and text indexing. Understanding these data structures can significantly enhance your ability to work with string data in diverse applications.

6.3 Fenwick Tree and Segment Tree

Fenwick Tree and Segment Tree are specialized data structures used for efficient range queries and updates on arrays. In this section, we'll delve into Fenwick Tree and Segment Tree, their characteristics, and their applications.

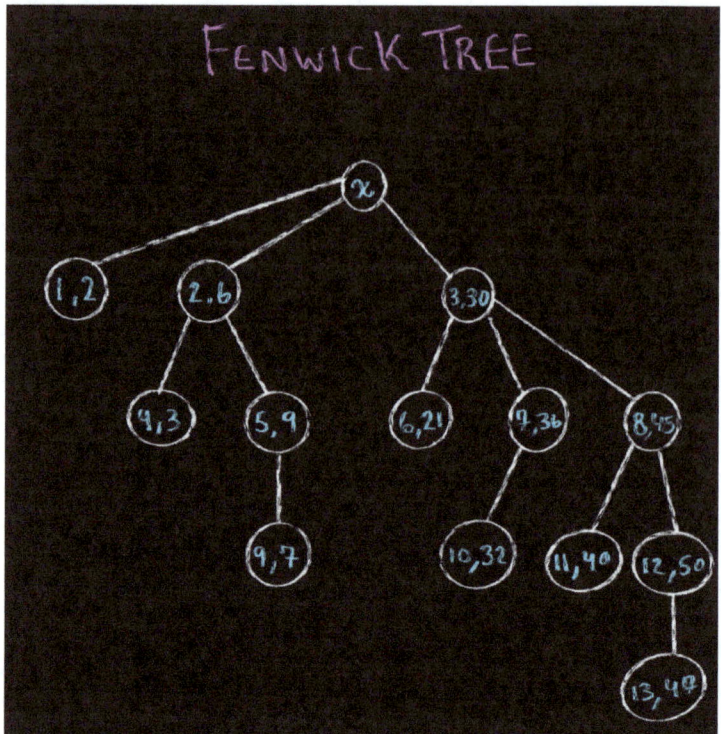

Figure 6.19

6.3.1 Understanding Fenwick Tree

A Fenwick Tree, also known as a Binary Indexed Tree (BIT), is a versatile data structure designed for efficiently performing cumulative range queries and updates on an array. It's particularly useful when dealing with large arrays in scenarios where you need to compute prefix sums, range sums, and single element updates.

6.3.2 Key Characteristics of a Fenwick Tree

1. Binary Tree Structure A Fenwick Tree is represented as a binary tree, where each node stores the cumulative sum of a range of elements in the original array.

2. Efficient Range Queries Fenwick Trees excel in computing prefix sums or ranges sums in O(log n) time complexity, where n is the number of elements.

3. Efficient Updates Updates (incrementing or decrementing) individual elements of the array are also efficient with O(log n) time complexity.

6.3.3 Building a Fenwick Tree

To build a Fenwick Tree, you initialize an array of zeros and populate it by iteratively updating elements to represent the cumulative sums. The process leverages binary representation to efficiently find and update relevant nodes in the tree.

6.3.4 Performing Range Queries and Updates

To compute a range sum or prefix sum, you navigate the Fenwick Tree by following a specific pattern. Updates are done similarly by traversing the tree and updating nodes in the path.

6.3.5 Understanding Segment Tree

A Segment Tree is a more complex data structure that also supports range queries and updates on an array. It's versatile and can handle a variety of queries beyond range sums, such as finding minimum or maximum values within a range. Segment Trees are commonly used in competitive programming and various algorithmic tasks.

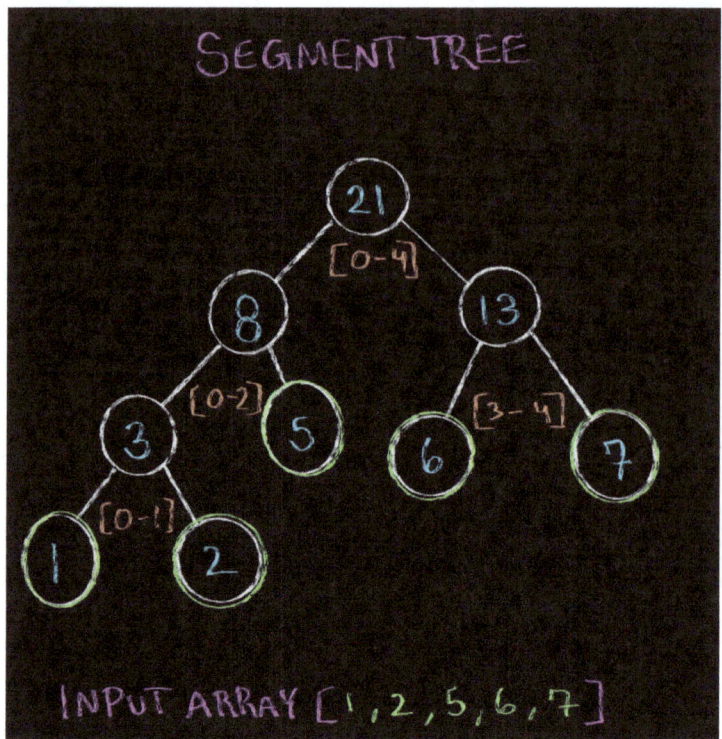

Figure 6.20

6.3.6 Key Characteristics of a Segment Tree

1. Balanced Binary Tree Structure A Segment Tree is represented as a balanced binary tree, where each node stores information about a specific range of elements in the original array.

2. Versatile Queries Segment Trees can be customized to support a wide range of queries, including range sum, minimum value, maximum value, and more.

3. Efficient Range Queries and Updates Querying and updating elements in a Segment Tree are performed with O(log n) time complexity.

6.3.7 Building a Segment Tree

Constructing a Segment Tree involves dividing the array into smaller segments and recursively building a tree from those segments. The information stored in each node depends on the type of query the tree is designed to answer.

6.3.8 Performing Range Queries and Updates

Segment Trees are designed to efficiently handle a variety of queries, such as finding the sum, minimum, or maximum value in a given range. Queries are executed by traversing the tree and combining information from relevant nodes.

6.3.9 Applications

Fenwick Trees are commonly used in scenarios like finding cumulative sums in dynamic arrays, and they are a valuable tool in competitive programming.

Segment Trees are versatile and are widely used in various algorithmic tasks, including range queries and updates for different types of data.

6.3.10 Conclusion

Fenwick Tree and Segment Tree are specialized data structures that are highly efficient for performing range queries and updates on arrays. Fenwick Trees are particularly useful for cumulative sum calculations, while Segment Trees offer versatility in solving a variety of range query problems. By understanding and utilizing these data structures, you can significantly improve your ability to efficiently process and analyze array-based data.

6.4 Spatial Data Structures

Spatial data structures are specialized data structures designed to efficiently organize and query geometric and spatial data. They play a crucial role in various applications, including geographic information systems (GIS), computer graphics, and computer-aided design (CAD). In this section, we'll explore spatial data structures, their key characteristics, and their applications.

6.4.1 Understanding Spatial Data Structures

Spatial data structures are used to manage and retrieve spatial objects in multidimensional spaces efficiently. These objects can be points, lines, polygons, or complex geometries. Spatial data structures allow for the organization of data based on their geometric properties, enabling fast queries for tasks such as searching for nearby objects, range queries, and intersection tests.

6.4.2 Key Characteristics of Spatial Data Structures

1. Multidimensional Organization Spatial data structures organize data in multiple dimensions, accommodating various spatial attributes and types of data.

2. Efficient Search They provide efficient search and retrieval operations, allowing for quick spatial queries.

3. Hierarchical Structure Many spatial data structures use hierarchical or tree-based structures to divide the space into smaller regions, making queries more manageable.

4. Balanced Partitioning Spatial data structures often aim to balance the division of space to maintain efficiency in query operations.

6.4.3 Common Spatial Data Structures

1. Quadtree A hierarchical spatial data structure that divides space into four equal quadrants recursively. It's efficient for point queries and range searches.

2. Octree An extension of the quadtree to three-dimensional space, dividing it into octants. Octrees are used in 3D applications, such as 3D modeling and computer graphics.

3. R-tree A tree-based spatial data structure that organizes objects in multidimensional space. It's used for range queries, nearest-neighbor searches, and indexing spatial databases.

4. K-d tree A binary tree structure that partitions space using axis-aligned hyperplanes. It's valuable for nearest-neighbor searches and multidimensional data.

5. Bounding Volume Hierarchy (BVH) A hierarchical structure used in computer graphics to optimize rendering and collision detection.

6.4.4 Applications

Geographic Information Systems (GIS) Spatial data structures are essential for managing and querying geographic data, including maps, satellite imagery, and location-based services.

Computer Graphics They are used for rendering, collision detection, and spatial indexing in 3D graphics and game development.

Database Systems Spatial data structures play a vital role in spatial databases, allowing efficient retrieval of spatial data in applications like real estate, urban planning, and logistics.

Robotics and Autonomous Systems Spatial data structures enable robots and autonomous vehicles to navigate, avoid obstacles, and plan paths.

6.4.5 Conclusion

Spatial data structures are fundamental tools for efficiently handling and analyzing spatial and geometric data. They offer a range of capabilities for spatial queries, making them indispensable in various applications, from geographic information systems to computer graphics and beyond. By understanding and utilizing these structures, you can leverage the power of spatial data for a wide array of tasks and applications.

Chapter 7: Searching and Sorting Algorithms

In this chapter, we'll explore essential searching and sorting algorithms, foundational techniques that are crucial in programming and data structure manipulation. We'll discuss various search algorithms, including linear and binary search, as well as sorting algorithms like bubble sort, selection sort, insertion sort, merge sort, and quick sort.

7.1 Linear and Binary Search

Search algorithms are fundamental in computer science and are essential for finding specific items or values in a collection of data. Two common search algorithms are Linear Search and Binary Search. In this section, we'll explore these search algorithms, their characteristics, and when to use them.

7.1.1 Understanding Linear Search

Linear Search, also known as Sequential Search, is the simplest search algorithm. It works by sequentially checking each element in a collection, one by one, until the desired item is found or the entire collection is traversed. Linear Search is straightforward and easy to implement but can be inefficient for large datasets.

7.1.2 Key Characteristics of Linear Search

1. Sequential Scanning Linear Search examines each item in the collection in order, from the beginning to the end.

2. No Assumption Linear Search does not rely on any specific ordering of the data; it can be used for both sorted and unsorted collections.

3. Time Complexity In the worst case, Linear Search has a time complexity of $O(n)$, where n is the number of elements in the collection.

7.1.3 When to Use Linear Search

Linear Search is suitable for small datasets or when you do not have any prior information about the arrangement of data. It is also applicable when the data is not frequently updated, as it has a linear time complexity.

7.1.4 Understanding Binary Search

Binary Search, also known as Logarithmic Search, is a more efficient search algorithm that works by repeatedly dividing the search interval in half. It requires the collection to be sorted, allowing for a much faster search than Linear Search. Binary Search is commonly used in scenarios where the data is sorted.

7.1.4.1 Binary Search Sample Code in Python

```python
def binary_search(arr, target):
    left = 0
    right = len(arr) - 1

    while left <= right:
        mid = left + (right - left) // 2

        if arr[mid] == target:
            return mid  # Element found, return its index

        if arr[mid] < target:
            left = mid + 1
        else:
            right = mid - 1

    return -1  # Element not found

numbers = [4, 8, 15, 16, 23, 42]
target = 16

result = binary_search(numbers, target)

if result != -1:
    print(f"Element found at index {result}")
else:
    print("Element not found in the list")
```

Figure 7.1

7.1.4.1 Binary Search Sample Code in C++

```cpp
#include <iostream>
#include <vector>

int binarySearch(const std::vector<int>& arr, int target) {
    int left = 0;
    int right = arr.size() - 1;

    while (left <= right) {
        int mid = left + (right - left) / 2;

        if (arr[mid] == target) {
            return mid; // Element found, return its index
        }

        if (arr[mid] < target) {
            left = mid + 1;
        } else {
            right = mid - 1;
        }
    }

    return -1; // Element not found
}

int main() {
    std::vector<int> numbers = {4, 8, 15, 16, 23, 42};
    int target = 16;

    int result = binarySearch(numbers, target);

    if (result != -1) {
        std::cout << "Element found at index " << result << std::endl;
    } else {
        std::cout << "Element not found in the array" << std::endl;
    }

    return 0;
}
```

Figure 7.2

7.1.5 Key Characteristics of Binary Search

1. Divide and Conquer Binary Search systematically divides the
search interval in half and compares the target value with the middle
element to determine the next search interval.

2. Requires Sorted Data Binary Search only works on sorted collections.

3. Time Complexity Binary Search has a time complexity of O(log n) in the worst case, making it significantly faster for large datasets compared to Linear Search.

7.1.6 When to Use Binary Search

- Binary Search is ideal for situations where the data is sorted and needs to be searched efficiently. It is commonly used in databases, libraries, and file systems to quickly locate items based on keys.

7.1.7 Comparing Linear and Binary Search

	Linear Search	Binary Search
Search Algorithm	Sequentially examines each item	Divides and conquers the search space
Data Order	Sorted or unsorted	Sorted
Time Complexity	O(n)	O(log n)
Applicability	Suitable for small datasets and unsorted data	Ideal for large datasets and sorted data

Table 7.1

7.1.8 Conclusion

Linear Search and Binary Search are fundamental search algorithms with distinct characteristics and use cases. Linear Search is simple and suitable for small or unsorted datasets, while Binary Search is highly efficient for large, sorted datasets. By understanding when to use each of these search algorithms, you can make informed decisions when searching for specific items or values in your data.

7.2 Bubble, Selection, Insertion Sort

Sorting algorithms are essential in computer science and data processing. They enable us to arrange elements in a specific order, making it easier to search and retrieve data efficiently. In this section, we'll explore three fundamental sorting algorithms: Bubble Sort, Selection Sort, and Insertion Sort.

7.2.1 Understanding Bubble Sort

Bubble Sort is one of the simplest sorting algorithms. It repeatedly steps through the list, compares adjacent elements, and swaps them if they are in the wrong order. The pass-throughs continue until no more swaps are needed, indicating that the list is sorted. Bubble Sort is straightforward to implement but not very efficient, especially for large datasets.

7.2.2 Key Characteristics of Bubble Sort

1. Comparison and Swap Bubble Sort compares adjacent elements and swaps them if they are in the wrong order.

2. Passes Through the List It performs multiple passes through the list, with each pass potentially reducing the number of out-of-order elements.

3. Time Complexity Bubble Sort has a time complexity of $O(n^2)$ in the worst case, making it less suitable for large datasets.

7.2.3 Understanding Selection Sort

Selection Sort is another straightforward sorting algorithm. It divides the input list into two sublists: the sorted part and the unsorted part. It repeatedly selects the minimum (or maximum) element from the unsorted part and moves it to the end of the sorted part. Selection Sort is simple to understand and has a consistent time complexity.

7.2.4 Key Characteristics of Selection Sort

1. Dividing into Sorted and Unsorted Parts Selection Sort maintains two sublists—one sorted and one unsorted.
2. Finding the Minimum (or Maximum) It selects the minimum (or maximum) element from the unsorted part and appends it to the sorted part.
3. Time Complexity Selection Sort has a time complexity of $O(n^2)$ in the worst case.

7.2.5 Understanding Insertion Sort

Insertion Sort builds the sorted list one element at a time, inserting each new element into its correct position within the sorted part of the list. It is efficient for small datasets and nearly sorted data but becomes less practical for large datasets.

7.2.6 Key Characteristics of Insertion Sort

1. Building the Sorted Part Insertion Sort builds the sorted part of the list incrementally by inserting each new element.
2. Insertion Process For each new element, it compares it with the elements in the sorted part and inserts it at the appropriate position.
3. Time Complexity Insertion Sort has a time complexity of $O(n^2)$ in the worst case but performs better with partially sorted data.

7.2.7 Comparing Sorting Algorithms

Sorting Algorithms	Key Characteristics	Time Complexity
Bubble Sort	Repeatedly compares and swaps adjacent elements	$O(n^2)$
Selection Sort	Divides the list into sorted and unsorted parts. Selects the	$O(n^2)$

	minimum (or maximum) element	
Insertion Sort	Builds the sorted part incrementally, inserts elements	O(n^2)

Table 7.2

7.2.8 When to Use Each Sorting Algorithm

Bubble Sort, Selection Sort, and Insertion Sort are suitable for small datasets and simple implementation scenarios.

Bubble Sort and Selection Sort are often used for educational purposes but are less efficient for large datasets.

Insertion Sort can be practical when the data is mostly sorted, making it well-suited for small to moderately sized datasets.

7.2.9 Conclusion

Bubble Sort, Selection Sort, and Insertion Sort are fundamental sorting algorithms, each with its own set of characteristics and use cases. While they may not be the most efficient sorting methods for large datasets, understanding these algorithms provides valuable insights into sorting concepts and computer science fundamentals. In practice, for large datasets, more efficient sorting algorithms such as Quick Sort and Merge Sort are preferred.

7.3 Merge Sort, Quick Sort

Merge Sort and Quick Sort are efficient sorting algorithms that offer significant performance advantages over simpler sorting methods like Bubble Sort or Selection Sort. In this section, we'll explore these two sophisticated sorting algorithms, their characteristics, and their applications.

7.3.1 Understanding Merge Sort

Merge Sort is a divide-and-conquer sorting algorithm that recursively divides the unsorted list into smaller sublists until each sublist consists of a single element. Then, it merges these sublists in a sorted manner. Merge Sort is known for its stability and consistent performance.

7.3.2 Key Characteristics of Merge Sort

1. Divide and Conquer Merge Sort divides the list into smaller sublists until each sublist contains one element (the base case).

2. Merging It then merges these sublists in a sorted order, creating larger sorted sublists until the entire list is sorted.

3. Efficiency Merge Sort has a time complexity of O(n log n) in the worst case, making it efficient for large datasets.

4. Stability Merge Sort is a stable sorting algorithm, which means that the relative order of equal elements is preserved.

7.3.3 Understanding Quick Sort

Quick Sort is another efficient divide-and-conquer sorting algorithm. It selects a 'pivot' element from the list and partitions the other elements into two sublists—those less than the pivot and those greater than the pivot. The process is repeated on the sublists until the entire list is sorted. Quick Sort is known for its speed and is often used as the default sorting algorithm in many programming languages.

7.3.4 Key Characteristics of Quick Sort

1. Pivot Selection Quick Sort selects a pivot element from the list to partition the data.

2. Partitioning It divides the list into two sublists based on the pivot, where elements less than the pivot are on one side and elements greater than the pivot are on the other side.

3. Recursion The algorithm is applied recursively to the sublists.

4. Efficiency Quick Sort has an average time complexity of $O(n \log n)$ in the average case, making it one of the fastest sorting algorithms.

5. In-Place Sorting Quick Sort can be performed in-place with a low memory overhead, making it suitable for large datasets.

7.3.5 Comparing Merge Sort and Quick Sort

Sorting Algorithm	Key Characteristics	Time Complexity	Memory Usage
Merge Sort	Divide-and-conquer, stable	$O(n \log n)$	Requires additional memory for merging
Quick Sort	Divide-and-conquer, in-place	$O(N \log n)$ on average, $O(n^2)$ in worst case	Low memory usage

Table 7.3

7.3.6 When to Use Each Sorting Algorithm

Merge Sort is preferred when stability is important or when the dataset cannot be sorted in place.

Quick Sort is a versatile and efficient sorting algorithm suitable for most scenarios. It is often the preferred choice for sorting large datasets, thanks to its low memory usage and average-case time complexity.

7.3.7 Conclusion

Merge Sort and Quick Sort are sophisticated sorting algorithms that provide efficient and stable sorting solutions for a wide range of scenarios. Merge Sort excels when stability and additional memory usage are not primary concerns. Quick Sort, on the other hand, offers a versatile and fast sorting solution, making it a popular choice for a variety of applications. Understanding and using these algorithms can significantly enhance your ability to work with and process data efficiently.

Chapter 8: Algorithm Design Techniques

In this chapter, we'll explore algorithm design techniques that go beyond basic data structures and enable you to solve complex problems efficiently. We'll discuss divide and conquer, greedy algorithms, dynamic programming, and backtracking, providing insights into when and how to apply these strategies in Python and C++.

8.1 Divide and Conquer

Divide and Conquer is a fundamental algorithmic paradigm that involves solving a problem by breaking it down into smaller subproblems, solving the subproblems, and then combining their solutions to solve the original problem. It is a powerful and versatile approach used in various algorithmic applications.

8.1.1 Key Concepts of Divide and Conquer

1. Divide The problem is divided into smaller subproblems that are similar to the original problem but simpler in nature. This division continues until the subproblems become trivial and easily solvable.

2. Conquer Each subproblem is solved independently, often by applying the same divide-and-conquer approach recursively. If the subproblems are simple enough, they are solved directly.

3. Combine The solutions to the subproblems are combined to obtain the solution to the original problem. The combining step may involve merging, aggregating, or applying other operations depending on the problem.

8.1.2 Applications of Divide and Conquer

Divide and Conquer is widely used in various computational tasks and algorithms, including:

Sorting Algorithms Algorithms like Merge Sort and Quick Sort use divide and conquer to efficiently sort data.

Search Algorithms Binary search is a classic example of a divide-and-conquer search algorithm.

Mathematical Computations Divide and conquer can be applied to compute mathematical functions, such as exponentiation and matrix multiplication.

Data Structures Recursive data structures, like balanced trees and heaps, are often built using divide and conquer.

Parallel and Distributed Computing Divide-and-conquer paradigms are valuable in parallel and distributed computing to harness the power of multiple processors or nodes.

Optimization Problems Divide and conquer can be used to solve optimization problems by recursively dividing the problem space and finding optimal solutions.

8.1.3 Characteristics of Divide and Conquer

1. Recursion Divide-and-conquer algorithms are typically expressed using recursive functions that repeatedly divide and solve subproblems until the base case is reached.

2. Efficiency Divide and conquer often leads to efficient algorithms because it can reduce the problem size significantly at each step.

3. Parallelization The divide-and-conquer approach is inherently parallelizable, making it suitable for parallel and distributed computing environments.

4. Optimality Some divide-and-conquer algorithms, like Merge Sort, are optimal in terms of time complexity for the problems they address.

8.1.4 Challenges in Divide and Conquer

1. Identifying Subproblems Decomposing the problem into subproblems requires a deep understanding of the problem's structure and the ability to identify meaningful subproblems.

2. Overhead Recursive function calls and combining subproblem solutions can introduce overhead in terms of time and space complexity.

8.1.5 Conclusion

Divide and Conquer is a powerful and versatile algorithmic paradigm that finds applications in various domains of computer science and computational mathematics. By breaking complex problems into smaller, more manageable subproblems and applying a divide-and-conquer approach, you can design efficient algorithms to tackle a wide range of challenges. Understanding this paradigm is a valuable asset for algorithm designers and computer scientists.

8.2 Greedy Algorithms

Greedy algorithms are a class of algorithms that make locally optimal choices at each step in the hope of finding a globally optimal solution to a problem. Greedy algorithms are simple to understand and often provide efficient solutions for a wide range of problems. In this section, we'll delve into the principles of greedy algorithms, their characteristics, and their common applications.

8.2.1 Key Principles of Greedy Algorithms

1. Greedy Choice Property Greedy algorithms make a series of choices at each step, selecting the best option according to a certain criterion. The choice is made without considering the consequences of the choice on future steps.

2. Optimal Substructure Greedy algorithms rely on the principle that solving a problem optimally involves solving its subproblems

optimally. This property is crucial for the success of greedy approaches.

8.2.2 Characteristics of Greedy Algorithms

1. Simplicity Greedy algorithms are typically simple to understand and implement, making them accessible for a wide range of problems.

2. Efficiency Greedy algorithms often provide efficient solutions, as they do not explore all possibilities but make local choices that aim to lead to a globally optimal result.

3. Optimality While greedy algorithms do not guarantee the globally optimal solution in all cases, they often provide solutions that are very close to the optimum.

8.2.3 Applications of Greedy Algorithms

Greedy algorithms are applied to a variety of problems, including:

Minimum Spanning Tree Algorithms like Kruskal's and Prim's find the minimum spanning tree in a connected graph.

A Minimum Spanning Tree (MST) is a fundamental concept in graph theory and network design. It is a subset of the edges of an undirected, connected graph that includes all the vertices of the graph while minimizing the total edge weight or cost. The primary goal of an MST is to connect all nodes with the minimum possible total edge weight, making it a tree (acyclic and connected).

Here are some key characteristics and properties of a Minimum Spanning Tree:

1. **Connectivity**: An MST ensures that all vertices in the original graph are connected. This means that there is a path between any two vertices in the MST.

2. **Acyclicity**: An MST is acyclic, which means it has no cycles or loops. This property is essential because it ensures that the tree structure remains a tree.

3. **Minimization**: An MST minimizes the sum of edge weights or costs. This is usually measured in terms of the weight of edges, and the goal is to find the MST with the smallest possible total weight.

4. **Uniqueness**: In general, a graph may have multiple MSTs, especially when some edges have the same weight. However, the overall weight of these MSTs will be the same.

5. **Cut Property**: The cut property states that for any cut (a partition of the vertices into two disjoint sets), the minimum-weight edge that crosses the cut belongs to the MST.

6. **Optimality**: The edges of the MST are selected optimally to minimize the total weight, which is why it is called a minimum spanning tree.

Minimum Spanning Trees have various applications in real-world problems, including network design, such as laying out cables to connect a set of cities at minimal cost, or designing efficient transportation routes. They are also used in designing efficient electrical circuits and clustering in data analysis.

Algorithms like Kruskal's algorithm and Prim's algorithm are commonly used to find Minimum Spanning Trees in a graph. These algorithms iteratively select edges while ensuring that the tree remains connected and acyclic and that the total weight is minimized.

Shortest Path Dijkstra's algorithm is a greedy approach used to find the shortest path between nodes in a graph with non-negative edge weights.

The shortest path in a graph refers to the path between two vertices (nodes) in a weighted graph that has the smallest sum of edge weights. In other words, it is the path with the minimum cost or distance between two points in the graph. Shortest path problems are fundamental in graph theory and have numerous practical applications, including route planning, network design, and optimization.

There are two main types of shortest path problems:

1. **Single-Source Shortest Path (SSSP)**:In this problem, you are given a source node and want to find the shortest paths from that source node to all other nodes in the graph. The most common algorithm for solving the SSSP problem is Dijkstra's algorithm, which works for graphs with non-negative edge weights. Another algorithm for SSSP is the Bellman-Ford algorithm, which can handle graphs with negative edge weights.

2. **All-Pairs Shortest Path (APSP)**: In this problem, you want to find the shortest paths between all pairs of nodes in the graph. The Floyd-Warshall algorithm is a classic solution for the APSP problem. It works for both positive and negative edge weights, but it doesn't work with negative cycles.

Key concepts and properties related to shortest paths in a graph include:

- **Path Length**: The length of a path is the sum of the weights of the edges in the path. For unweighted graphs, the path length is simply the number of edges in the path.

- **Optimality**: Shortest path algorithms find paths that are optimal in terms of minimizing the path length.

- **Directed and Undirected Graphs**: Shortest path algorithms can be applied to both directed and undirected graphs. In directed graphs, the direction of the edges matters in finding the shortest path.

- **Negative Weights**: When dealing with graphs with negative edge weights, it's important to consider the possibility of negative cycles, as they can impact the correctness and efficiency of some algorithms.

- **Applications**: Shortest path problems have applications in various domains, such as GPS navigation, network routing, game AI (e.g., pathfinding in video games), and optimization problems.

In summary, finding the shortest path in a graph is a fundamental problem with many real-world applications. The choice of algorithm and approach depends on the specific characteristics of the graph, such as whether it's weighted, directed, or contains negative weights or cycles. The goal is to find the most efficient path between two nodes while minimizing the associated cost or distance.

Huffman Coding Greedy algorithms are used to generate efficient variable-length codes for data compression.

Huffman coding, created by David A. Huffman in 1952, is a popular and widely used algorithm for lossless data compression. It is used to compress data, such as text or other types of files, in a way that minimizes the amount of storage or transmission bandwidth required. Huffman coding is particularly efficient for data with non-uniform symbol frequencies, as it assigns shorter binary codes to more frequent symbols and longer codes to less frequent symbols.

Here are the key components and characteristics of Huffman coding:

1. **Frequency-Based Encoding**:
   - Huffman coding operates on the principle that more frequent symbols in the data are assigned shorter binary codes, while less frequent symbols are assigned longer codes.
   - It builds a binary tree, known as the Huffman tree, in which symbols are placed as leaf nodes, and the path from the root to a leaf node represents the binary code for that symbol.

2. **Huffman Tree**:

- The Huffman tree is a binary tree with the following properties:
- Each leaf node of the tree represents a symbol from the input data.
- Internal nodes have no associated symbol and are formed by merging the two nodes with the lowest frequencies.
- The path from the root to each leaf node forms the binary code for that symbol.
- The tree is constructed through a process of iteratively merging nodes with the lowest frequencies until only one node remains, which becomes the root of the tree.

3. **Variable-Length Codes**:
- Huffman coding results in variable-length codes, meaning that different symbols can have codes of different lengths.
- Shorter codes are assigned to more frequent symbols, which makes the representation more efficient for common symbols.

4. **Efficiency**:
- Huffman coding is efficient for compressing data with non-uniform symbol frequencies, as it minimizes the average code length.
- It guarantees that no other prefix of a binary code is the prefix of another code, ensuring that the encoded data can be uniquely decoded.

5. **Decoding**:
- To decode a Huffman-encoded message, the Huffman tree is used to traverse the tree from the root to a leaf node, following the binary code. When a leaf node is reached, the corresponding symbol is output, and the traversal continues from the root of the tree.

6. **Lossless Compression**:
- Huffman coding is a lossless compression technique, meaning that the original data can be perfectly reconstructed from the encoded data.

Huffman coding is widely used in various applications, including text compression in file formats like ZIP and GZIP, image compression (e.g., JPEG), and data transmission in network protocols. It is considered one of the most efficient lossless compression algorithms, particularly when applied to data with varying symbol frequencies, as it minimizes the overall storage or transmission size while allowing for lossless recovery of the original data.

Knapsack Problem The greedy approach is applied to solve variations of the knapsack problem, where items have values and weights, and the goal is to maximize value within a weight constraint.

The Knapsack problem is a well-known combinatorial optimization problem that can be described as follows:

Given a set of items, each with a weight and a value, determine the maximum value that can be obtained by selecting a subset of the items while ensuring that the total weight of the selected items does not exceed a given capacity.

In more formal terms:

- There are n items, each with a weight, w[i], and a value, v[i], for i = 1 to n.
- There is a knapsack with a maximum weight capacity, W.
- You want to select a subset of items to maximize the total value, subject to the constraint that the sum of the weights of the selected items does not exceed the knapsack's capacity.

Mathematically, the Knapsack problem can be expressed as an optimization problem:

Maximize $\Sigma(v[i] * x[i])$, where i = 1 to n
Subject to: $\Sigma(w[i] * x[i]) \leq W$, where i = 1 to n

120

x[i] = 0 or 1, indicating whether the item i is selected (x[i] = 1) or not (x[i] = 0).

The Knapsack problem is a classic NP-hard problem, which means that there is no known polynomial-time algorithm to solve it optimally for large instances. However, various algorithms and techniques can be used to approximate the solution or find the optimal solution for smaller instances. Dynamic programming and greedy algorithms are commonly employed to solve different variations of the Knapsack problem.

The Knapsack problem has numerous practical applications, including resource allocation, project selection, portfolio optimization, and cutting stock problems in manufacturing. It serves as a fundamental problem in combinatorial optimization and computational complexity theory.

Interval Scheduling Greedy algorithms can be used to solve problems involving scheduling and selecting non-overlapping intervals with maximum value or efficiency.

Interval scheduling is a classic problem in the context of greedy algorithms and is often used to illustrate the greedy approach. It involves selecting the maximum number of non-overlapping intervals from a set of intervals, such that each selected interval does not overlap with any others. The goal is to find a schedule that maximizes the utilization of a resource over time while ensuring that no two intervals overlap.

Here's the formal description of the Interval Scheduling problem:

1. You are given a set of n intervals, each with a start time (si) and an end time (ei), where i = 1 to n.

2. You want to find a subset of these intervals such that no two intervals in the subset overlap.

3. The objective is to select as many intervals as possible.

The greedy algorithm for solving the Interval Scheduling problem works as follows:

1. Sort the intervals in ascending order of their end times.

2. Start with an empty set of selected intervals.

3. Iterate through the sorted intervals. For each interval, add it to the selected set if it does not overlap with any previously selected interval.

The key insight in the greedy approach is that selecting the interval with the earliest end time maximizes the availability of the resource for subsequent intervals. By continually selecting intervals with the earliest end times and ensuring they do not overlap with each other, you maximize the number of intervals that can be scheduled without conflicts.

Interval scheduling has practical applications in scheduling and resource allocation problems, such as:

- Classroom scheduling: Assigning classrooms to different classes to maximize resource utilization while avoiding class time conflicts.
- Job scheduling: Scheduling tasks or jobs to run on a computer system without overlap.
- Conference room booking: Scheduling meetings or events in available conference rooms without time conflicts.

The greedy algorithm for interval scheduling is efficient and often used as a foundational example of how greedy algorithms work. It finds a near-optimal solution for this specific problem and provides insight into the general principles of the greedy approach.

8.2.4 Challenges in Greedy Algorithms

1. Greedy Choice Selection Identifying the appropriate criterion for making the greedy choices is crucial. A suboptimal choice at any step can lead to a suboptimal overall solution.

2. Proving Correctness Demonstrating the correctness of a greedy algorithm and ensuring that it consistently provides near-optimal solutions can be challenging.

8.2.5 Conclusion

Greedy algorithms are a valuable and efficient tool for solving a wide range of problems. They rely on making locally optimal choices at each step, with the hope of achieving a globally optimal result. While not suitable for all problems, understanding the principles and applications of greedy algorithms is essential for algorithm designers and problem solvers, as they can provide elegant and efficient solutions to complex challenges.

8.3 Dynamic Programming

Dynamic Programming is a powerful algorithmic technique used to solve problems by breaking them down into smaller overlapping subproblems and storing the solutions to these subproblems to avoid redundant work. It is particularly effective for optimization problems and problems with recursive structures. In this section, we'll explore the principles of dynamic programming, its key characteristics, and its applications.

8.3.1 Key Principles of Dynamic Programming

1. Optimal Substructure Dynamic programming relies on the principle that solving a problem optimally involves solving its subproblems optimally. The optimal solution to the overall problem can be constructed from the optimal solutions to its subproblems.

2. Overlapping Subproblems Dynamic programming problems exhibit overlapping subproblems, where the same subproblems are encountered multiple times during the computation. To avoid redundant work, dynamic programming algorithms store and reuse solutions to these subproblems.

8.3.2 Characteristics of Dynamic Programming

1. Efficiency Dynamic programming is designed to optimize the computational efficiency of solving problems by avoiding redundant calculations through the use of memoization or tabulation.

2. Top-Down vs. Bottom-Up Approaches Dynamic programming can be applied using either a top-down approach (recursion with memoization) or a bottom-up approach (iterative tabulation). The choice of approach depends on the problem and the preferred implementation style.

3. Memory Usage Dynamic programming may require additional memory to store solutions to subproblems. The trade-off between time and space complexity should be considered when applying dynamic programming.

8.3.3 Applications of Dynamic Programming

Dynamic programming is applied to a wide range of problems, including:

Fibonacci Sequence Dynamic programming efficiently computes Fibonacci numbers and other recursive sequences.

Shortest Path Problems Algorithms like Dijkstra's and Floyd-Warshall use dynamic programming to find the shortest paths in graphs.

Sequence Alignment Dynamic programming is used in bioinformatics to align sequences, such as DNA sequences, to identify similarities.

Optimization Problems Many optimization problems, such as the knapsack problem and the traveling salesman problem, are efficiently solved using dynamic programming.

Dynamic Time Warping Dynamic programming is used for measuring the similarity between two time series, which is applied in speech recognition and gesture recognition.

8.3.4 Challenges in Dynamic Programming

1. Identifying Subproblems Decomposing the problem into meaningful subproblems is crucial for the success of dynamic programming. This step requires a deep understanding of the problem's structure.

2. Optimal State Transition Determining the rules or transitions between subproblems that lead to an optimal solution can be challenging, as it depends on the specific problem.

8.3.5 Conclusion

Dynamic programming is a powerful technique for solving problems by dividing them into smaller overlapping subproblems and efficiently reusing their solutions. It is widely used in algorithm design, optimization, and solving complex problems. Understanding the principles of dynamic programming and its applications is essential for algorithm designers and problem solvers, as it provides a structured approach to tackling a wide range of challenges.

8.4 Backtracking

Backtracking is an algorithmic technique used to solve problems by exploring all possible solutions incrementally and efficiently. It is particularly useful for problems with multiple decision points and where a brute-force approach is impractical. In this section, we'll delve into the principles of backtracking, its key characteristics, and its applications.

8.4.1 Key Principles of Backtracking

1. Exploration of Solution Space Backtracking involves systematically exploring the solution space by making decisions and undoing them when necessary.

2. Pruning Unpromising Paths As the algorithm progresses, it prunes paths that are unlikely to lead to a valid solution, optimizing the search.

8.4.2 Characteristics of Backtracking

1. Depth-First Search Backtracking typically employs a depth-first search strategy to explore the solution space. It traverses as far as possible along one path before backtracking to explore other paths.

2. Recursion or Iteration Backtracking can be implemented using recursion or iteration, depending on the problem and programming language.

3. Space Efficiency Backtracking algorithms are often memory-efficient, as they do not require storing all possible solutions simultaneously.

8.4.3 Applications of Backtracking

Backtracking is applied to a variety of problems, including:

N-Queens Problem Backtracking is used to find all possible ways to arrange N queens on an N×N chessboard without attacking each other.

Sudoku Solving Backtracking algorithms are applied to solve Sudoku puzzles by incrementally filling cells with numbers while ensuring no conflicts.

Maze Solving Backtracking is used to find paths through mazes and labyrinths, exploring all possible routes.

Subset and Permutation Generation Backtracking is employed to generate all subsets, permutations, or combinations of a given set of elements.

Cryptarithmetic Puzzles Backtracking is used to solve cryptarithmetic puzzles, where letters represent digits and a valid assignment needs to be found.

8.4.4 Challenges in Backtracking

1. Identifying Decision Points Recognizing the decision points in a problem, where choices need to be made, can be challenging.

2. Efficiency and Pruning Efficiently pruning unpromising paths to reduce the search space is crucial to ensure that backtracking algorithms are practical.

8.4.5 Conclusion

Backtracking is a valuable algorithmic technique for solving problems with multiple decision points and where exhaustive search is required. It offers a structured and systematic approach to exploring all possible solutions while efficiently pruning unpromising paths. Understanding the principles and applications of backtracking is essential for algorithm designers and problem solvers, as it provides a powerful tool for solving complex and combinatorial problems.

Chapter 9: Advanced Topics

In this chapter, we'll explore advanced topics related to data structures and algorithms. We'll cover B-trees and AVL trees, dive deeper into graph algorithms, explore algorithm optimizations, and discuss real-world applications of data structures and algorithms in Python and C++.

9.1 B-trees and AVL Trees

B-Trees and AVL Trees are two types of self-balancing tree structures used in computer science and databases to efficiently manage and store large amounts of data. These tree structures are designed to maintain balance and ensure efficient operations for insertion, deletion, and retrieval. In this section, we'll explore the principles, characteristics, and applications of B-Trees and AVL Trees.

9.1.1 Understanding B-Trees

A B-Tree is a balanced tree data structure that is designed to maintain balance and optimize disk-based storage. B-Trees have the following key characteristics:

1. Balanced Structure B-Trees are balanced trees, meaning that the height of the tree is kept as small as possible, ensuring efficient search, insertion, and deletion operations.

2. Degree B-Trees are defined by a parameter called the degree, which determines the minimum and maximum number of children a node can have.

3. Sorted Data B-Trees store data in a sorted order within each node, which allows for efficient search and range queries.

4. Efficient for Disk Storage B-Trees are commonly used in databases and file systems because they are optimized for efficient

disk-based storage, reducing the number of disk accesses required for data retrieval.

9.1.2 Applications of B-Trees

B-Trees are widely used in various applications, including:

Databases B-Trees are the basis for indexing data in database management systems, allowing for efficient search and retrieval of records.

File Systems B-Trees are used in file systems to efficiently manage and access files and directories.

Storage Systems B-Trees are employed in storage systems to manage the allocation and location of data blocks.

In-Memory Databases B-Trees are also used in in-memory databases, where efficient data management is crucial.

9.1.3 Understanding AVL Trees

An AVL Tree is a type of self-balancing binary search tree that ensures the height of the left and right subtrees of any node differs by at most one. AVL Trees have the following key characteristics:

1. Balanced Height AVL Trees maintain a balanced height, which guarantees that search, insertion, and deletion operations have a time complexity of O(log n).

2. Rotations AVL Trees use rotations to rebalance the tree after insertions and deletions to maintain their balance property.

3. Self-Balancing AVL Trees are self-balancing, meaning that after each operation, the tree ensures that it remains balanced.

4. Ordered Structure Similar to other binary search trees, AVL Trees store data in a sorted order, allowing for efficient search operations.

9.1.4 Applications of AVL Trees

AVL Trees are used in applications that require efficient data retrieval and maintenance of balance, including:

Databases AVL Trees can be used for indexing in databases, especially when efficient search operations are crucial.

Text Editors AVL Trees are used in text editors for efficient text searching and manipulation.

File Systems AVL Trees can be applied in file systems for maintaining directory structures.

9.1.5 Conclusion

B-Trees and AVL Trees are essential self-balancing tree structures used in various applications to efficiently manage and store data. B-Trees are designed for optimized disk-based storage and are widely used in databases and file systems, while AVL Trees are self-balancing binary search trees used in applications requiring balanced data structures. Understanding these tree structures and their applications is important for data management and algorithm design in computer science and information technology.

9.2 Algorithm Optimizations

Algorithm optimization is a crucial aspect of computer science and software development. It involves improving the performance, efficiency, and resource utilization of algorithms to meet specific requirements or constraints. In this section, we'll explore the principles of algorithm optimization, various optimization techniques, and their applications.

9.2.1 Key Principles of Algorithm Optimization

1. Efficiency Algorithm optimization aims to make algorithms more efficient by reducing time complexity, space complexity, or both. The goal is to achieve faster execution and minimize resource usage.

2. Trade-Offs Optimization often involves trade-offs between time and space complexity. Improving one aspect may come at the expense of the other, and the choice depends on the specific problem and requirements.

3. Benchmarking Effective optimization relies on benchmarking and performance measurement. Comparing the performance of different algorithm versions is essential to assess improvements.

9.2.2 Optimization Techniques

1. Time Complexity Reduction

- Algorithmic Improvements: Enhancing algorithm design through clever data structures, dynamic programming, and efficient search and traversal strategies.
- Parallelization: Utilizing parallel computing to execute tasks concurrently and speed up algorithms.
- Caching and Memoization: Storing and reusing results of expensive function calls to avoid redundant calculations.

2. Space Complexity Reduction

- Data Compression: Reducing memory usage through data compression techniques, such as bit manipulation and data encoding.
- In-Place Algorithms: Modifying algorithms to operate with minimal additional memory.
- Streaming Algorithms: Processing data streams with limited memory by making decisions on-the-fly.

3. Algorithmic Variations

- Heuristic and Approximation Algorithms: Using heuristics and approximation algorithms to find near-optimal solutions quickly.
- Randomized Algorithms: Introducing randomness to algorithms to achieve a balance between time and space efficiency.

4. Hardware and Platform Optimization

- Utilizing Specialized Hardware: Taking advantage of hardware accelerators, GPUs, and other specialized hardware for specific tasks.
- Memory Hierarchy Management: Optimizing memory access patterns to make efficient use of caches and main memory.

9.2.3 Applications of Algorithm Optimization

Algorithm optimization is applied in various domains, including:

- Database Management: Optimizing database queries and indexing to enhance data retrieval and processing efficiency.
- Image and Video Processing: Optimizing algorithms for image and video compression, enhancement, and analysis.
- Artificial Intelligence and Machine Learning: Improving training and inference algorithms for deep learning models to reduce execution time and resource consumption.
- Network Routing and Protocol Optimization: Enhancing routing algorithms and network protocols to reduce latency and improve data transfer efficiency.
- Game Development: Optimizing rendering, physics, and AI algorithms in video game development to achieve smooth gameplay and realistic graphics.

9.2.4 Challenges in Algorithm Optimization

1. Identifying Bottlenecks Identifying the performance bottlenecks in an algorithm or system is often the first step in optimization.

2. Complexity and Trade-Offs Achieving optimization can be complex, involving trade-offs between various factors like time, space, and maintainability.

3. Testing and Validation Careful testing and validation are essential to ensure that optimizations do not introduce errors or unexpected behaviors.

9.2.5 Conclusion

Algorithm optimization is an essential skill in computer science and software development. It aims to make algorithms more efficient in terms of time and space complexity while considering trade-offs and constraints. Optimization techniques are applied across a wide range of domains to improve the performance and resource utilization of algorithms, ultimately leading to faster and more efficient software systems. Understanding and applying these techniques is critical for developing high-quality software and solving complex computational challenges.

9.3 Real-world Applications

Data structures and algorithms are fundamental components of computer science and play a crucial role in a wide range of real-world applications. In this section, we'll explore how data structures and algorithms are applied in practical scenarios to solve complex problems and optimize processes.

9.3.1 Information Retrieval and Search Engines

Data Structures Search engines like Google use complex data structures such as inverted indexes, suffix trees, and B-Trees to efficiently index and search through vast amounts of web content.

Algorithms Ranking algorithms, like PageRank, analyze link structures to determine the relevance and importance of web pages.

9.3.2 Social Media and Recommendations

Data Structures Social media platforms employ data structures to store and manage user profiles, relationships, and user-generated content.

Algorithms Recommendation algorithms, like collaborative filtering, use data from user interactions to suggest content and connections.

9.3.3 Financial Analysis and Trading

Data Structures Financial systems use data structures to manage large datasets of historical and real-time market data.

Algorithms Algorithms for technical analysis, pattern recognition, and risk management are used in trading systems.

9.3.4 Healthcare and Medical Research

Data Structures Patient records and medical data are managed using data structures to enable efficient retrieval and analysis.

Algorithms Machine learning algorithms are used for tasks such as disease diagnosis, drug discovery, and genetic analysis.

9.3.5 Transportation and Logistics

Data Structures Logistics companies use data structures to optimize routes, track shipments, and manage inventory.

Algorithms Routing algorithms, like Dijkstra's and A*, help determine the most efficient paths for delivery and transportation.

9.3.6 Natural Language Processing and AI

Data Structures Text data is processed using data structures such as tries, hash tables, and graphs to extract information and perform sentiment analysis.

Algorithms Machine learning and deep learning models are applied for tasks like language translation, chatbots, and voice recognition.

9.3.7 Robotics and Autonomous Systems

Data Structures Robotics systems use data structures to represent sensor data and environment maps.

Algorithms Path planning and control algorithms enable autonomous robots to navigate and interact with their surroundings.

9.3.8 Genomics and Bioinformatics

Data Structures Genomic data, DNA sequences, and protein structures are managed using specialized data structures to enable efficient analysis.

Algorithms Sequence alignment algorithms and phylogenetic tree construction are used to study genetic relationships and analyze evolutionary patterns.

9.3.9 Gaming and Virtual Reality

Data Structures Game engines utilize data structures to manage 3D environments, game objects, and player interactions.

Algorithms Physics simulations, collision detection, and pathfinding algorithms enhance gameplay experiences.

9.3.10 Energy and Environment

Data Structures Environmental monitoring systems collect data from various sensors and use data structures to analyze trends and patterns.

Algorithms Predictive models and optimization algorithms are applied to manage energy consumption and reduce environmental impact.

9.3.11 Conclusion

Data structures and algorithms are not abstract concepts limited to theoretical computer science but are practical tools with real-world applications. These applications span diverse domains, from information retrieval and social media to finance, healthcare, transportation, and many others. Understanding how to leverage data structures and algorithms in practical scenarios is essential for solving complex problems, optimizing processes, and creating innovative solutions that benefit society and industry.

Chapter 10: Python and C++ Best Practices

In this final chapter, we'll focus on best practices for working with data structures and algorithms in Python and C++. You'll learn how to write clean, maintainable code, test and debug your implementations, optimize for performance, and manage memory effectively.

10.1 Code Style and Documentation

- We'll start by discussing the importance of code style and documentation in Python and C++. Clean and well-documented code is easier to maintain and understand.
- You'll learn about coding conventions, naming conventions, and documentation practices in both languages.

10.2 Testing and Debugging

- Effective testing and debugging are essential to ensure the correctness and reliability of your data structure implementations.
- We'll explore testing frameworks, techniques for writing unit tests, and strategies for debugging common issues.

10.3 Performance Optimization

- Performance matters, especially when dealing with large datasets and time-critical applications. We'll discuss strategies for optimizing code in Python and C++.
- You'll learn about profiling, algorithm analysis, and techniques like memoization and caching to improve performance.

10.4 Memory Management

- Managing memory efficiently is crucial, especially in C++. We'll delve into memory management practices and tools.

- You'll gain insights into memory allocation, pointers, smart pointers, and techniques to prevent memory leaks and manage resources.

List of Figures

Data Structures and AI: Leveraging AI with Data Structures

Artificial Intelligence (AI) and Data Structures are two powerful domains in computer science that, when combined, can unlock new possibilities and efficiencies. In this section, we'll explore how AI can be used with data structures and provide insights into how to integrate them effectively.

1. AI and Data Structures: A Powerful Synergy

AI encompasses a wide range of techniques and algorithms designed to enable machines to learn, reason, and make decisions. Data structures, on the other hand, are fundamental for organizing and manipulating data efficiently. Combining the two can lead to remarkable results:

2. Data Preparation and Feature Engineering
Data preparation and feature engineering are critical steps in machine learning and data science. They involve cleaning and transforming raw data into a format that can be effectively used by machine learning models. Data structures and AI can play a significant role in these processes. Here's more information along with some code examples in Python:

2.1 Data Preparation with Data Structures and AI

a. Data Collection Collecting data from various sources, which can be stored and organized using data structures such as lists, arrays, or data frames.

b. Data Cleaning Cleaning and preprocessing data to handle missing values, outliers, and inconsistencies.

141

```
import pandas as pd

# Create a DataFrame to store and clean data
data = pd.DataFrame({'feature1': [1, 2, None, 4, 5],
                     'feature2': [0.5, 0.7, 0.3, None, 0.9]})
data_cleaned = data.dropna()
```

c. Data Integration Combining data from different sources or datasets using data structures like lists or dictionaries.

```
# Combine two lists into one
list1 = [1, 2, 3]
list2 = [4, 5, 6]
combined_list = list1 + list2
```

d. Data Transformation Transforming data using various techniques, including scaling, normalization, and one-hot encoding.

```
from sklearn.preprocessing import StandardScaler

# Scale the features using StandardScaler
scaler = StandardScaler()
scaled_data = scaler.fit_transform(data_cleaned)
```

2.2 Feature Engineering with Data Structures and AI

Feature engineering involves creating new features or transforming existing ones to improve model performance. Here's how data structures and AI can be applied:

a. Creating New Features Use data structures to create new features based on domain knowledge or algorithms.

```
# Create a new feature by combining existing features
data_cleaned['feature_sum'] = data_cleaned['feature1'] \
                              + data_cleaned['feature2']
```

b. Text Data Processing Process text data using data structures like dictionaries or sets to build features such as bag-of-words or TF-IDF.

```
from sklearn.feature_extraction.text import CountVectorizer

# Create a bag-of-words representation of text data
corpus = ['This is the 1st document.', 'This document is the 2nd document.']
vectorizer = CountVectorizer()
X = vectorizer.fit_transform(corpus)
```

c. Time Series Feature Extraction Extract time-based features from datetime data.

```
# Extract year, month, and day as new features
data_cleaned['year'] = data_cleaned['date'].dt.year
data_cleaned['month'] = data_cleaned['date'].dt.month
data_cleaned['day'] = data_cleaned['date'].dt.day
```

d. Dimensionality Reduction Use dimensionality reduction techniques like Principal Component Analysis (PCA) to reduce feature dimensions.

```
from sklearn.decomposition import PCA

# Apply PCA for dimensionality reduction
pca = PCA(n_components=2)
X_pca = pca.fit_transform(scaled_data)
```

e. Feature Selection Select important features using AI techniques like feature importance scores.

```
from sklearn.ensemble import RandomForestClassifier

# Train a model to get feature importance scores
model = RandomForestClassifier()
model.fit(X, y)
feature_importance = model.feature_importances_
```

f. Feature Scaling Use data structures like arrays or data frames to store and scale features.

```
from sklearn.preprocessing import MinMaxScaler

# Scale features to a specified range
scaler = MinMaxScaler(feature_range=(0, 1))
scaled_features = scaler.fit_transform(X)
```

g. Feature Extraction from Images Utilize AI models like
Convolutional Neural Networks (CNNs) for image feature
extraction.

```
from tensorflow.keras.applications import VGG16
from tensorflow.keras.preprocessing import image
from tensorflow.keras.applications.vgg16 import preprocess_input

# Load a pre-trained CNN model
model = VGG16(weights='imagenet', include_top=False)

# Preprocess an image and extract features
img_path = 'image.jpg'
img = image.load_img(img_path, target_size=(224, 224))
img = image.img_to_array(img)
img = preprocess_input(img)
features = model.predict(img)
```

In data preparation and feature engineering, combining data
structures and AI techniques helps you effectively process,
transform, and create features from your data to improve the
performance of machine learning models. These examples
demonstrate the synergy between data structures and AI in these
essential tasks.

3. Optimization and Search Algorithms

Artificial Intelligence (AI) techniques can be powerful tools for
optimization and search algorithms. They can help find the best
solutions in complex problem spaces, often where brute force search
is impractical. Below, I'll provide an overview of some AI methods
for optimization and search along with Python code examples:

a. Genetic Algorithms (GAs)

Genetic algorithms mimic the process of natural selection to find approximate solutions to optimization and search problems.

```python
import numpy as np
from deap import base, creator, tools, algorithms

# Define a fitness function
def fitness_function(individual):
    return sum(individual),  # Single objective optimization

creator.create("FitnessMin", base.Fitness, weights=(1.0,))
creator.create("Individual", list, fitness=creator.FitnessMin)

toolbox = base.Toolbox()
toolbox.register("attr_bool", np.random.randint, 0, 2)
toolbox.register("individual", tools.initRepeat, \
                 creator.Individual, toolbox.attr_bool, n=10)
toolbox.register("population", tools.initRepeat, list, toolbox.individual)

toolbox.register("evaluate", fitness_function)
toolbox.register("mate", tools.cxTwoPoint)
toolbox.register("mutate", tools.mutFlipBit, indpb=0.05)
toolbox.register("select", tools.selTournament, tournsize=3)

population = toolbox.population(n=50)
algorithms.eaMuPlusLambda(population, toolbox, mu=10, lambda_=40, cxpb=0.7,\
                          mutpb=0.2, ngen=50, stats=None, halloffame=None)
```

b. Particle Swarm Optimization (PSO)

PSO algorithms optimize problems by simulating the behavior of swarms of birds or fish to find the global optimum.

```python
!pip install pyswarm
import pyswarm

# Define the objective function to minimize
def objective_function(x):
    return sum(x**2)

lb = [-10, -10, -10]
ub = [10, 10, 10]
x_opt, f_opt = pyswarm.pso(objective_function, lb, ub)
```

c. Simulated Annealing

Simulated annealing is a probabilistic optimization technique inspired by the annealing process in metallurgy.

145

```
import numpy as np
import scipy.optimize as opt

# Define the objective function
def objective_function(x):
    return sum(x**2)

x0 = np.array([1.0, 2.0, 3.0])
result = opt.basinhopping(objective_function, x0)
```

d. Tabu Search

Tabu search is a heuristic search method that can be applied to discrete and combinatorial optimization problems.

```
import numpy as np
import scipy.optimize as opt

# Define the objective function
def objective_function(x):
    return sum(x**2)

x0 = np.array([1.0, 2.0, 3.0])
result = opt.basinhopping(objective_function, x0)
```

e. Metaheuristic Algorithms

Various metaheuristic algorithms, such as Ant Colony Optimization (ACO), Particle Swarm Optimization (PSO), and Genetic Algorithms (GA), can be applied to a wide range of optimization and search problems.

Python Example (Ant Colony Optimization)

```python
from ant_colony_optimization import ACO

# Define problem-specific parameters, such as pheromone levels, distances, etc.
parameters = {
    "pheromone_initial": 1.0,
    "alpha": 1.0,
    "beta": 3.0,
    "evaporation": 0.5,
    "max_iterations": 100
}

# Create an instance of the ACO solver
aco = ACO(parameters)

# Solve the optimization problem
best_solution, best_cost = aco.solve()
```

These are just a few examples of how AI techniques can be used for optimization and search algorithms. Depending on the specific problem and requirements, different AI algorithms may be more suitable. Python provides libraries and tools for implementing and experimenting with a wide range of optimization and search techniques.

4. Graph-based AI

Many AI applications, including social network analysis and recommendation systems, involve graph data. Data structures like adjacency lists or matrices are used to represent and traverse graphs.

AI algorithms like graph neural networks (GNNs) leverage graph structures to make predictions and decisions based on connectivity patterns.

Graph-based AI involves modeling problems as graphs and using various techniques to analyze and make decisions based on the graph structures. Here's an overview of graph-based AI and some Python examples:

a. Graph Representation
- In graph-based AI, problems are represented as graphs, which consist of nodes and edges.
- Nodes represent entities, while edges represent relationships between entities.

b. Graph Traversal
- Algorithms like Breadth-First Search (BFS) and Depth-First Search (DFS) can be used to traverse graphs.
- Python libraries like NetworkX and igraph provide tools for working with graphs.

Python Example (BFS using NetworkX)

```
import networkx as nx

G = nx.Graph()
G.add_edges_from([(1, 2), (1, 3), (2, 4), (3, 5), (4, 6)])

# Perform BFS traversal
bfs_order = list(nx.bfs_tree(G, source=1))
print("BFS traversal:", bfs_order)
```

c. Shortest Path Algorithms
  - Algorithms like Dijkstra's algorithm and the Bellman-Ford algorithm can be used to find the shortest path in graphs.

Python Example (Dijkstra's Algorithm using NetworkX)

```
import networkx as nx

G = nx.Graph()
G.add_weighted_edges_from([(1, 2, 3), (1, 3, 5),\
                           (2, 4, 2), (3, 5, 4), (4, 6, 1)])

# Find the shortest path using Dijkstra's algorithm
shortest_path = nx.shortest_path(G, source=1, target=6, weight='weight')
print("Shortest path:", shortest_path)
```

d. Graph Neural Networks (GNNs)

- GNNs are neural networks designed to work with graph-structured data.
- They are used for tasks like node classification, link prediction, and graph classification.

Python Example (Using PyTorch Geometric for Node Classification)

```python
!pip install torch_geometric
import torch
import torch_geometric
from torch_geometric.nn import GCNConv
from torch_geometric.datasets import Planetoid
import torch.nn.functional as F

# Load a graph dataset
dataset = Planetoid(root='/tmp/Cora', name='Cora')

class GCN(torch.nn.Module):
    def __init__(self, dataset, num_hidden):
        super(GCN, self).__init__()
        self.conv1 = GCNConv(dataset.num_features, num_hidden)
        self.conv2 = GCNConv(num_hidden, dataset.num_classes)

    def forward(self, data):
        x, edge_index = data.x, data.edge_index
        x = self.conv1(x, edge_index)
        x = F.relu(x)
        x = F.dropout(x, training=self.training)
        x = self.conv2(x, edge_index)
        return F.log_softmax(x, dim=1)

# Train a GNN for node classification
model = GCN(dataset, num_hidden=16)
optimizer = torch.optim.Adam(model.parameters(), lr=0.01, weight_decay=5e-4)
model.train()
for epoch in range(200):
    optimizer.zero_grad()
    out = model(dataset[0])
    loss = F.nll_loss(out, dataset.y)
    loss.backward()
    optimizer.step()
```

e. Recommendation Systems

- Graph-based recommendation systems use graphs to model user-item interactions and make personalized recommendations.

Python Example (Using NetworkX for Recommendation)

```python
import networkx as nx
from networkx.algorithms import bipartite

G = nx.Graph()
G.add_edges_from([(1, 'A'), (1, 'B'), (2, 'B'), (2, 'C'), (3, 'A')])

# Create a bipartite graph for user-item interactions
B = nx.Graph(G)
user_nodes = [n for n, d in G.nodes(data=True) if d['bipartite'] == 0]
item_nodes = [n for n, d in G.nodes(data=True) if d['bipartite'] == 1]
user_item_graph = bipartite.weighted_projected_graph(B, user_nodes)

# Recommend items to a user
recommendations = list(user_item_graph['user1'])
print("Recommended items:", recommendations)
```

Graph-based AI provides a powerful framework for solving various problems, including recommendation systems, network analysis, and more. Python has several libraries and tools, such as NetworkX and PyTorch Geometric, that can be used to work with graphs and apply AI techniques to them.

5. Memory Efficiency

Using AI for memory efficiency with data structures involves optimizing data storage and manipulation to reduce memory usage. Here's more information on how to use AI for memory efficiency with data structures and Python examples:

5.1 Sparse Data Structures

Sparse matrices and data structures are used when dealing with datasets that have many zero or low-value entries. These data structures use less memory by storing only the non-zero values.

Python Example (Using Scipy Sparse Matrix)

```python
import scipy.sparse

# Create a sparse matrix
data = [1, 2, 3, 0, 0, 0, 4, 0, 5]
row_indices = [0, 0, 1, 2, 2, 2, 3, 4, 4]
col_indices = [0, 2, 1, 0, 1, 3, 2, 3, 4]

sparse_matrix = scipy.sparse.coo_matrix((data, (row_indices, col_indices)))
```

5.2 Streaming and On-Disk Data Storage

Instead of loading entire datasets into memory, process data in chunks and utilize on-disk storage to reduce memory usage.

Python Example (Streaming Data with Pandas)

```python
import pandas as pd

# Read and process data in chunks
chunk_size = 1000
for chunk in pd.read_csv('large_dataset.csv', chunksize=chunk_size):
    # Process the chunk
```

5.3 Data Generator Functions

Create data generator functions that yield data on-the-fly to avoid loading all data into memory simultaneously.

Python Example (Data Generator Function)

```python
def data_generator(data_file):
    with open(data_file, 'r') as file:
        for line in file:
            # Process and yield data from the file
            yield process_data(line)
```

5.4 Online Learning and Mini-Batching

Train machine learning models using online learning techniques, processing small mini-batches of data at a time.

Python Example (Mini-Batch Training with Scikit-Learn)

```python
from sklearn.linear_model import SGDClassifier

clf = SGDClassifier(loss='log', random_state=42)
batch_size = 32
for X_batch, y_batch in mini_batch_generator(X, y, batch_size):
    clf.partial_fit(X_batch, y_batch, classes=np.unique(y))
```

5.5 Data Augmentation

Generate augmented data on-the-fly during training, reducing the need to store augmented copies of the data.

Python Example (Data Augmentation with TensorFlow)

```python
import tensorflow as tf

# Create an image data augmentation pipeline
data_augmentation = tf.keras.Sequential([
    tf.keras.layers.RandomFlip("horizontal"),
    tf.keras.layers.RandomRotation(0.2),
    tf.keras.layers.RandomZoom(0.1)
])

# Apply data augmentation to an image
augmented_image = data_augmentation(original_image)
```

5.6 Memory-efficient Data Structures

Utilize memory-efficient data structures like data frames with smaller memory footprints, optimized for AI tasks.

Python Example (Using Pandas with Memory Optimization)

```python
import pandas as pd

# Read and optimize memory usage
df = pd.read_csv('large_dataset.csv')
df = df.astype({"column_name": "int16"})
```

These examples demonstrate how data structures and Python can be used to implement memory-efficient AI techniques. Employing sparse data structures, streaming data, using data generators, and optimizing memory usage with data frames can significantly reduce memory requirements when working with large datasets and machine learning models.

5.7 Real-time Decision Making

n applications like autonomous vehicles, IoT, and gaming, real-time decision-making is critical. Data structures are used to store and access large datasets quickly, enabling AI algorithms to make decisions in real-time.

Data structures like spatial data structures and k-d trees can be essential for tasks involving spatial data.

Real-time decision-making in AI involves making quick, automated decisions based on real-time data. Data structures play a crucial role in efficiently processing and managing the data required for these decisions. Here's more information on real-time decision-making with data structures and Python examples:

5.8 Queue Data Structures

Queues are essential for managing data in real-time processing. They ensure that data is processed in the order it is received.

Python Example (Using `queue` module)

```python
import queue

# Create a FIFO queue
data_queue = queue.Queue()

# Enqueue data in real-time
data_queue.put("Data 1")
data_queue.put("Data 2")

# Dequeue and process data
while not data_queue.empty():
    data = data_queue.get()
    process_data(data)
```

5.9 Circular Buffers

Circular buffers are efficient for real-time data collection and analysis. They maintain a fixed-size buffer for continuous data input.

Python Example (Using `collections` module)

```python
from collections import deque

# Create a circular buffer
data_buffer = deque(maxlen=100)

# Add data to the buffer in real-time
data_buffer.append("Data 1")
data_buffer.append("Data 2")

# Process data from the circular buffer
for data in data_buffer:
    process_data(data)
```

5.10 Data Streaming Libraries

Libraries like Kafka, RabbitMQ, and Apache Pulsar enable efficient real-time data streaming and message queuing.

Python Example (Using `pika` for RabbitMQ)

```python
import pika

# Connect to RabbitMQ
connection = pika.BlockingConnection(pika.ConnectionParameters('localhost'))
channel = connection.channel()

# Publish real-time data
channel.basic_publish(exchange='', routing_key='queue_name', body='Data 1')

# Consume and process data in real-time
def callback(ch, method, properties, body):
    process_data(body)

channel.basic_consume(queue='queue_name',\
                    on_message_callback=callback, auto_ack=True)
channel.start_consuming()
```

5.11 Real-time Decision Rules

Implement rules and decision logic to make automated decisions based on real-time data. Data structures can help manage these rules efficiently.

155

Python Example (Rule-Based Decision Making)

```python
def real_time_decision(data):
    if data['temperature'] > 30:
        return "Turn on cooling"
    elif data['humidity'] > 60:
        return "Activate dehumidifier"
    else:
        return "No action needed"

data = {'temperature': 32, 'humidity': 65}
decision = real_time_decision(data)
```

5.12 Stream Processing Frameworks

Stream processing frameworks like Apache Kafka Streams and Apache Flink are designed for real-time data analysis and decision-making.

Python Example (Using `pyflink` for Apache Flink)

```python
from pyflink.datastream import StreamExecutionEnvironment
from pyflink.table import StreamTableEnvironment

# Set up Flink environment
env = StreamExecutionEnvironment.get_execution_environment()
t_env = StreamTableEnvironment.create(env)

# Define real-time data processing logic
t_env.from_path('source_topic') \
    .filter("temperature > 30") \
    .select("action") \
    .insert_into('output_topic')

# Execute the Flink job for real-time decision-making
t_env.execute("Real-Time Decision Job")
```

Real-time decision-making with data structures and Python is crucial for various applications, including IoT, finance, fraud detection, and monitoring systems. Effective use of data structures, queues, circular buffers, and streaming libraries allows for efficient data handling and decision logic implementation in real-time environments.

5.13 Integrating AI with Data Structures

To effectively integrate AI with data structures, consider the following steps:

a. Data Preprocessing: Use data structures for efficient data preprocessing and cleaning. Arrays, trees, and hash tables can help with tasks such as filtering, imputing missing data, and normalizing features.

b. Model Selection: Choose AI models that are compatible with the data structures you plan to use. For example, graph-based data may be best suited for GNNs, while time series data could benefit from recurrent neural networks (RNNs).

c. Optimization: Utilize data structures to optimize AI algorithms. Heaps, priority queues, and dynamic programming techniques can help speed up optimization problems.

d. Real-time Processing: For applications requiring real-time decision-making, ensure that data structures are designed for low-latency access. Spatial data structures and memory-efficient representations are crucial.

e. Memory Management: AI models often demand substantial memory. Implement memory-efficient strategies, such as model quantization and data compression, using the appropriate data structures.

6 Conclusion

The synergy between AI and data structures opens up exciting opportunities to solve complex problems, optimize processes, and make data-driven decisions. By understanding how data structures and AI can complement each other, you can harness the full potential of both fields and build innovative AI applications that are efficient, reliable, and capable of handling large-scale data.

Bonus Exercises

1. Implement a Priority Queue for A* Search
   - Use a data structure that allows efficient extraction of the minimum element. Binary heaps are a common choice.

2. Implement a Quadtree for Spatial Data Partitioning
   - Recursively divide the space into quadrants and store spatial data in a tree structure.

3. Implement a Markov Decision Process (MDP) with a Hash Table
   - Use a hash table to store state-value pairs for efficient reinforcement learning.

4. Implement a Skip Graph for Fast Range Queries
   - Combine skip list and graph-like structures to enable fast range queries.

5. Implement a B*-Tree for Large-scale Database Indexing
   - Enhance B-Tree with features that support efficient indexing for large databases.

6. Implement a Particle Swarm Optimization (PSO) Algorithm with Linked Lists
   - Use linked lists to represent particles and their positions in the optimization space.

7. Implement a Bayesian Network with Decision Trees
   - Use decision trees as conditional probability distributions in the Bayesian network.

8. Implement a Genetic Algorithm with Graphs for Traveling Salesman Problem
   - Model the problem as a graph and apply genetic operators to find solutions.

9. Implement a Bloom Filter for Text Classification
   - Use a Bloom filter to quickly determine whether a feature exists in the classification model.

10. Implement a Neural Network with Hash Tables for Embeddings
   - Store embeddings in hash tables for efficient lookup during neural network training.

11. Implement a Graph Database for Social Network Analysis
   - Design a database structure that models social networks with nodes and relationships.

12. Implement a Reinforcement Learning Environment with an Array-Based Grid
   - Represent the environment as an array grid with states and rewards.

13. Implement a K-Means Clustering Algorithm with Heaps
   - Use heaps to efficiently manage points' assignments to clusters during K-Means.

14. Implement a Self-balancing AVL Tree for Text Autocompletion
   - Use an AVL tree to store and search for text completions.

15. Implement a Decision Tree for Recommender Systems
   - Create a decision tree with decision rules for making recommendations.

16. Implement a Bloom Filter with Hash Tables for Web Caching
   - Use a Bloom filter and hash tables for efficient web caching.

17. Implement a Game Tree with Minimax for Chess AI
   - Create a game tree for chess moves and apply the Minimax algorithm with alpha-beta pruning.

18. Implement a Hash Map for Natural Language Processing
   - Utilize a hash map to efficiently store and access linguistic resources like dictionaries and thesauri.

19. Implement a B+ Tree for Database Transaction Processing
   - Extend B+ Trees to manage database transactions efficiently.

20. Implement a Pathfinding Algorithm with a Fibonacci Heap
   - Use a Fibonacci heap to optimize pathfinding algorithms like Dijkstra's and Prim's.

21. Implement a Decision Support System with a Priority Queue
   - Use a priority queue to rank and manage decision options in a decision support system.

22. Implement a Decision Tree with Spatial Data for Geographic Information Systems (GIS)
   - Utilize a decision tree for classifying spatial data in GIS applications based on spatial attributes.

23. Implement a Genetic Algorithm for Job Scheduling with Graphs
   - Model job scheduling as a graph problem and apply genetic operators to optimize scheduling.

24. Implement a Neural Network with a Quadtree for Image Segmentation
   - Use a quadtree to divide images into regions and improve image segmentation in neural networks.

25. Implement a K-D Tree for Nearest Neighbor Search in Image Retrieval
   - Utilize a K-D tree for efficient nearest neighbor search when retrieving images.

26. Implement a Dynamic Programming Algorithm for Sequence Alignment with Hash Tables
- Use hash tables to optimize dynamic programming algorithms, such as sequence alignment in bioinformatics.

27. Implement a Heuristic Search Algorithm with B-Trees for Game Pathfinding
- Enhance game pathfinding algorithms by using B-Trees to store and search spatial data.

28. Implement a Self-organizing Map (SOM) for Clustering High-dimensional Data
- Apply a self-organizing map to cluster and visualize high-dimensional data efficiently.

29. Implement a Bayesian Network with Hash Tables for Information Retrieval
- Combine Bayesian networks with hash tables to improve information retrieval in AI applications.

30. Implement a Queue for BFS in Social Network Analysis
- Utilize a queue data structure for performing breadth-first search in social network analysis.

31. Implement a Genetic Algorithm for Automated Machine Learning Hyperparameter Tuning
- Apply a genetic algorithm to optimize the hyperparameters of machine learning models.

32. Implement a Particle Filter for Object Tracking with Linked Lists
- Use linked lists to manage particles and their states in object tracking for computer vision.

33. Implement a Hash Map for Text Summarization
- Utilize a hash map to efficiently store and access word frequency counts for text summarization.

34. Implement a Graph Database for Recommendation Systems
   - Create a graph database for storing and querying recommendation system data, modeling user-item interactions.

35. Implement a Quadtree for Collision Detection in Game Development
   - Apply a quadtree data structure to optimize collision detection algorithms in 2D game development.

36. Implement a Decision Tree with Reinforcement Learning for Game AI
   - Combine decision trees with reinforcement learning to create AI-controlled characters in game development.

37. Implement a Bloom Filter for Image Duplicate Detection
   - Use a Bloom filter to efficiently detect duplicate images in a large image database.

38. Implement a Neural Network with Hash Tables for Entity Recognition
   - Implement entity recognition in natural language processing using neural networks with hash tables.

39. Implement a Spatial Index with B-Trees for Geographic Information Systems (GIS)
   - Create a B-Tree-based spatial index to improve spatial data retrieval in GIS applications.

40. Implement a Genetic Algorithm for Feature Engineering
   - Use a genetic algorithm to automate the process of feature engineering in machine learning.

41. Implement a Self-balancing AVL Tree for Music Recommendation
   - Utilize an AVL tree for optimizing music recommendation systems based on user preferences and music attributes.

42. Implement a Stack for Depth-First Search in Knowledge Graphs
- Utilize a stack data structure to perform depth-first search in knowledge graphs, which model relationships and facts.

43. Implement a Genetic Algorithm with Multi-objective Optimization
- Use a genetic algorithm to solve problems with multiple objectives, such as optimizing for both speed and cost simultaneously.

44. Implement a Dijkstra's Algorithm for Shortest Path with Fibonacci Heap
- Use a Fibonacci heap to optimize Dijkstra's algorithm for finding the shortest path.

45. Implement a Genetic Algorithm for Function Optimization
- Apply a genetic algorithm to find the optimal parameters for a mathematical function.

46. Implement a Red-Black Tree for Symbol Table in Compiler Design
- Utilize a Red-Black tree to efficiently manage symbol tables during compiler design.

47. Implement a K-D Tree for Image Retrieval with Color Histograms
- Use a K-D tree to index and retrieve images based on color histograms.

48. Implement a B-tree for Database Indexing with Secondary Keys
- Enhance a B-tree to support secondary key indexing in databases.

49. Implement a Convolutional Neural Network (CNN) for Image Recognition
- Design a CNN architecture to recognize objects in images.

50. Implement a Trie for Autocompletion in Search Engines

- Create a trie data structure to offer efficient autocompletion suggestions in search engines.